Meta Selling

Meta Selling

Helping People to Buy A New & Better Way

DR. GARY S. GOODMAN

MEDIA

Published 2018 by Gildan Media LLC
aka G&D Media
www.GandDmedia.com

FIRST EDITION 2018

Front Cover design by David Rheinhardt of Pyrographx

Interior design by Meghan Day Healey of Story Horse, LLC

Library of Congress Cataloging-in-Publication Data is available upon request

ISBN: 978-1-7225-0037-5

10   9   8   7   6   5   4   3   2   1

Contents

Introduction 1

1 The 8th Wonder of The World:
   Getting Through Screening 13

2 How To Be A Mind Reader........................... 20

3 Getting People To Call You Back 27

4 Hurricane Gary—Making Actions
   Speak Louder... 32

5 What Does 'Responsibly Sourced' Mean? 42

6 What's It Going To Be:
   Yes, No, Or Maybe? 49

7 From Those Wonderful Folks
   That Gave You Pearl Harbor........................... 59

8 Should You Dress For Success
   Or Look Good? 70

9 Are You A Cherry Or A Pit?........................... 82

10 Finding Your Meta Selling Voice 94

11 How Much Money Will You Make? 97

12 But The SX-70 Is A Great Camera, Isn't It? 108

13 Controlling Your Self-Talk When You Fail 117

14 Meta Ways To Build Trust 127

15 Are You Trying To Sell Me Something? 134

16 "I Have A Little Problem On My Hands
        & Was Hoping You Could Help Me Out" 142

17 Do You Sincerely Want To Be Rich? 151

18 Smart Calls Versus Dumb Calls 161

19 Tones Talk! 173

20 What Is The Best Time To Sell? 183

21 Small Talk Makes Big Money! 191

22 The Art Of Selling 199

23 The Power Of Politeness:
        Sir, Ma'am, & I'm Sorry 209

24 Doing The Impossible:
        Selling Without Selling 217

        Afterword 222
        Index 223

Introduction

Helping People to Buy,
A New & Better Way

None other than the preeminent genius, Albert Einstein, said:

No problem can be solved from the same level of consciousness that created it.

Yet this is exactly the way we try to address challenges in selling.

Let's say a prospect is ducking your attempts to make contact, a perennial problem, right?

You sent emails, you phoned. You left voice mails. You texted. But in return, you're getting zilch, nada, nothing, no results. You're being "ghosted" as it's called in dating, mating, and social media.

What will your sales managers do day in and day out from that point? They will probably ask, "Hey, how are you doing with that Goodman account?"

"Can't reach him."

"Keep trying!" is the totally feckless advice you'll hear.

In other words, keep doing what isn't working in the hope it will suddenly work.

Your CRM system, perhaps Salesforce, will nudge you in the same direction, to relentlessly follow up. I've used systems that are programmed to get you to make a minimum of 12 follow-up attempts before you can justify returning the prospect to the general database.

You may have heard a customer's stall that you know in your bones makes the person not worth another ounce of your attention, but the software will make you waste 11 more attempts to prove what you already have intuited.

You've heard the definition of insanity that says continuing to do the same thing while expecting a different result is a mark of being crazy. If this is the case, 99.9% of today's sellers are bull-goose loony, as Ken Kesey tagged it, in his celebrated novel, *One Flew Over The Cuckoo's Nest*.

Our prescription for taking a win from a loss is to keep on losing, to do more of what is getting us nowhere.

I call this Level One Selling. It is the traditional way to get an order, or so we've been taught. Einstein and I agree: You need to get to a higher, better level to solve your sales problems.

That is Level Two: The Meta Selling Level.

When we Meta Sell, we are actually rising above the typical cut and thrust of everyday transactions. We're acknowledging and commenting on how and where we are going astray, in the hope of setting a new, better, and more cooperative course with our potential buyers.

Now, in fairness, Level One Selling persists for a reason. The Sales Establishment argues: "It works, that's why we do it!" There's some truth in that, but only a tiny grain of it.

What most sellers are doing works barely enough to justify its continuation and to shut out competing ways to sell that can be far more effective and efficient. Like a slot machine, it doesn't hook you on losing because it NEVER pays off. It pays on a staggered basis just enough to keep you glued to the machine.

It is perniciously addictive because it makes you inflate the value of your wins while underrating the impact of your losses. B.F Skinner, one of the most influential behavioral psychologists of all time, said: "intermittent reinforcement schedules" are the most addicting.

Translation: If you sold every single person you talked to, you grow bored. And you'd burn out quickly if you sold none of them. But a little winning, even if accompanied by a lot of losing will make you dial that next number, shoot out that email, or knock on the next prospect's door. This is our Level One Wiring.

Here are just two of Level One Selling's directives:

If a customer says no, don't believe it. "Buyers are liars," says a well-known and quite stupid cliché. Your job is to wear them down. They resist because they think that's their job. No one wants to be known as an "easy sale" or a "lay down!"

If a customer resists, use more force! Like Wonder Woman or Captain America wielding their shields, deflect the flack, and answer back with a volley of reasons to buy.

There have been authors that have detected something is wrong with these traditional do's and don'ts. They've tried to fix Level One selling by touting what they call "permission selling" and "consultative selling." I'll discuss these noble, but-still-inadequate remedies, later on.

Practitioners, people in the trenches, have also taken a shot at devising a better way to sell. I heard one of my clients, while training his office automation salespeople, quite refreshingly say:

"If prospects say 'no,' believe them!"

He went on to ask his initiates: "Why in the world would you ever want to talk to someone that sincerely doesn't want to talk with you?"

There is an answer to this question. The reason sellers have been so willing to waste their time is that they've tacitly been told that's what their job description is. They stand around in airports, in office lobbies, killing time. They twiddle their thumbs while on hold when they phone, and stay past quitting time in the hope that a promised order will be emailed in.

If your time is worthless, what difference does it make if you kill it? It was DOA when you were hired.

Certain companies only hire uber-competitive ex-athletes for their sales teams. They instill a take-no-prisoners approach that can be summed up this way: "If buyers push you, you push back."

It could be called, Smash-Mouth Selling. Frankly, it's injurious to everyone.

Let me give you a quick, recent example of doing it a far better, alternative way, using Meta Selling.

One of my clients in Chicago was ducking my calls. I tried reaching him without results. Instead of over-using the same media, the phone, email, text messages, I decided to use a different, far more customized means.

I Google-Earthed his business address and scanned his building and the structures around it. I found there is an Autozone dealer nearby.

Heck, I've bought a bunch of stuff from my local Autozone, so they owe me. (That's what I told myself.)

Anyway, I'm from Chicago, from the same area where this Autozone and my client are located.

I phoned the Autozone and asked for the manager. I told him I'm from the neighborhood originally and I can't reach my client. I'm worried something happened to him. His phone is not working. Maybe he went out of business, or moved.

He's two-doors down from you.

Could you please walk over there and see what's happening? His name is Paul Smith and if he's there would you tell him I'm trying to reach him and ask him to call me?

Several minutes later, the manager came back onto the line and beamed. "He's there! He said he would call you."

And that's exactly what happened. Victory! Success!

Why? I literally got above the problem. I solved it from a different level.

That's the "Meta" in action. I launched myself into orbit via Google's satellite imagery and peered down at my client's situation. I deputized someone, a stranger to me but a neighbor to him to look in on my client and report back to me.

I improvised a new medium of assisted selling in order to overcome the resistance I was facing with conventional, Level One calling and emailing.

Meta Selling acknowledges the fact that we must emerge from the cocoon of constraints in conventional business persuasion, changing the form, metamorphosing, so we can fly above the problems we're having, fixing them in the process.

I pitched a nationwide school of high fashion modeling. Then there was silence. Repeatedly, I left phone messages. At one point, I muttered to myself, this isn't working.

I decided to write a letter, that's correct, putting ink on paper and sending it though the conventional mail. Addressed to the president, the headline read:

Where Did We Go Wrong?

I acknowledged right away that I must have erred in the process of managing their interest in my services. I said, because I'm in sales and marketing I need to improve, as well.

Even more valuable than hiring me I would treasure their feedback. Please inscribe in the lines below how I missed the mark, and I'll be very grateful.

The president phoned me and promptly hired me to speak at their national convention. It was a delightful and lucrative program.

What did my Meta Communication, "Where Did We Go Wrong?" say?

It said I blew it—please help me out. Even though I teach selling skills, I guess I'm not perfect at selling. Kindly, make me better!

This is a role reversal. I turned the tables. I took off my expert hat and donned the dunce cap. I became the novice, again.

I extricated us from the traditional sales roles that were failing us. By doing so, we adopted new roles that resulted in a win-win relationship.

People use Meta Communication and Meta Persuasion all the time, mostly without knowing it.

I was standing in the UPS store last week when a woman hurriedly came in, saw the boss and said, "I hate to ask you this, but can you please tell me where the nearest FedEx office is?"

He gladly revealed TWO nearby locations where she could give her business to his competitors!

I must say, I've observed this grouchy guy for years and I've never known him to be anything but a taciturn type that is awful at doing customer service. Yet he rolled over and purred for her!

You're at a grocery store and someone cuts in line ahead of you. You'll probably seethe at the unfairness. But if he or she asks, "May I cut in front of you because I have to get back to my car?" typically, you'll be glad to wave them ahead.

Research has shown folks like you and I will yield our spots, patiently earned, to anyone bearing a "because." In the example provided, the line-cutter needed to get back to her car and didn't have to explain further.

"Because" is the smart Meta part to the message, in the same way "I hate to do this" was the Meta message in the UPS store.

When we have enough self-awareness, enough emotional intelligence to know that we could be coming across poorly or at sub-optimal effectiveness, we can volunteer effective explanations in advance:

"I'm sorry if I sound a little on edge, but a car just ran a red light and nearly crashed into me!"

"No problem; that can really be upsetting. You okay?"

"Yeah, thanks."

The first speaker is aware that he may be coming off a little edgy, sending signals his recipient doesn't expect to process.

By pointing it out, he is demonstrating sensitivity and quite practically avoiding resistance and conflict. He's saying:

"It's not you; it's me, and please don't think I'm communicating brusquely with you because I don't like you. You see, based on what just happened to me, I can't help myself, so kindly forgive me."

Yesterday, I wrote the following note to a business contact that "blows hot and cold," seemingly interested in doing business with me one day, but distancing himself the very next day. Frankly, I don't know if he's interested or not.

Hello _____,

I've been trying to connect with you but I can't reach you and I'm concerned there's something amiss.

How should I proceed? There are two schools of thought:

(1) Desist: Don't try to reach people that don't want to be reached. Or,

(2) Persist: You don't know what's going on with them, and their silence can be misinterpreted.

Please advise me: Is it (1) or (2)? Or, maybe (3)!

Many thanks.

Best,

Gary

(818) 970-GARY (4279)

What are the advantages in sending this kind of note? Let's examine the Meta-Messages I'm embedding.

First, I'm saying I'm confused. Second, I'm asking for help to quickly eliminate the confusion. Third, I'm implying this isn't a good way to do business and he has a duty to help me to determine what's going on.

If he doesn't, he'll be wasting my time and his. I'll keep calling and writing and he'll keep avoiding. Where is the productivity in that?

All of this is being communicated, politely. That's the key. And I have to say I have achieved dramatic results using Meta-Messages in selling.

Don't underestimate the power in asking for help. One of the best sales presentations I ever used started this way:

"Hello, this is Gary Goodman with the Goodman Organization. How are you? That's good. The reason I'm calling is I have a little problem on my hands and I was hoping you might help me out."

A huge proportion of listeners will respond to this overture with the sweet and generous reply:

"Well, I will if I can; what's going on?"

Note, they're saying this to an utter stranger. I have relatives that won't give me the time of day, but this example shows how nice many normal, everyday people are when approached the right way.

Now it's up to me to tell them how my problem can help them to take advantage of the situation.

Normally, sellers don't talk about their problems. We're taught to focus on the client's. But by putting my incapacity out there right away, saying something isn't quite right with me, I meta-communicate that this conversation is going to go in a different direction than they're used to.

And this is good and disarming, because people believe they know the sales "drill" all too well. It has become predictable, but that is a gift if you know how to Meta Sell.

Meta Selling can help you to re-fashion the tacit, customary rules of engagement:

"Now that we've made contact you might expect me to follow-up with you until the end of time to earn your business. I'd like to, but this isn't efficient. If I waste our time then my prices go up and ultimately you pay for my inefficiency, and that's not fair, is it? So, please join with me in making this process leaner & easier. Here's how. If you're not interested, please say so right away and I'll back off. The next best thing to getting a green light is getting a red light. It tells me what to do, fair enough?"

I've just provided a few illustrations in this Introduction. There is far more to come.

These high cash-value techniques will earn you more business and grateful customers. You'll relate to prospects in refreshingly new and better ways.

Much of the hostile, adversarial sales tension will evaporate.

You'll accelerate your relationships and bond with your clients as you never have, before.

Specifically, in the material that follows I'm going to share with you my 20-second sales pitch. I'll challenge you to find the persuasion in it, which isn't at all obvious. This text is totally denuded of any "salesy" quality. Yet it is overwhelmingly successful.

It helped me to earn millions of dollars and to sell the smartest and stodgiest people on earth.

It's a gem of Meta Selling, and you can use it, too. It will save you oodles of time and really cut to the chase.

And I promise you that you won't sound like anyone else that is competing for the prospect's business!

We'll address some of the hardest challenges in selling, from penetrating voice mail and human screening to deciding who is worth pursuing and who is simply wasting your time.

You'll learn to become an expert "Re-animator," reviving dead and dormant accounts with ease and grace.

You'll be amazed at the specificity of my examples. In many cases, I'll point out not only the words to use, but also the specific tones and timing for expressing them.

I've been there. While my suggestions are thoroughly powerful on a theoretical level, because I hold a Ph.D. in Communication from USC, they are grounded in my years of practical selling experience.

When I've been at my very best, I've employed Meta Selling precepts and practices. Now, for the first time, I've codified them so you can benefit, as well.

Get ready for a brand new way to do the same-old! You're going to love this stuff!

1

The 8th Wonder of The World: Getting Through Screening

Remember that scene in the original Star Wars movie when Obi-Wan Kenobi waves his hand in front of a Stormtrooper and calmly states, "These are not the droids you're looking for."

He used what is referred to as a Jedi Mind Trick.

The trooper accepts his statement as fact and lets the droids pass without further question.

This is our exact goal with call screeners. We need them to pass us on to a buyer or to an influencer.

For this to happen, they need to change their default setting from perceiving us as threats. In a very short amount of time we have to convince them that we belong inside the fort they're guarding.

If we over-explain we'll seem amateurish and undeserving. If we try to break in forcefully, they'll blow us off the path. Being snarky and defensive will also result in tears.

If we permit them to interrogate us, we'll definitely lose.

They have a script and it works. It consists of these parts:

Hello, Alpha company; how may I direct your call?

Who's calling?

Is she expecting your call?

And what's this about?

Does she know you?

She's not available.

I'll tell her you called.

Goodbye.

This should sound familiar. It is baked into practically every screener, everywhere.

Maybe one in 100,000 sellers pause to consider what a losing proposition it is to permit this script to enter the conversation. They just succumb to it, and then get waylaid.

One in a million salespeople actually introduce an alternative call path for screening.

We're going to do that, here. It constitutes one of Gary's Greatest Hits. I'm really proud of this because it works.

It works? How do I know?

I installed an appointment–setting unit at a division of Xerox. Their purpose was to arrange first meetings with top brass at Fortune 1000 companies. They sold million-dollar hardware and software bundles.

On single calls, they were able to set meetings with the CEO at Boeing and other top-tier organizations.

To get through call screening was the first order of business. I totally redesigned the protocol for doing it.

The first precept, and this is an unwritten Meta Selling notion, is if you want to get cooperation you need to offer cooperation, first.

So, instead of making screeners tease the information out of us about who we are and why we're phoning, we offered all the in formation, up-front.

"Hello, this is Gary Goodman with All Flakes Federal Supply. What's the name of the owner there, please?

I offered my name in advance. Operating on the idea that if I want information, someone's name, I need to volunteer mine. This creates transparency trust. I'm changing my stranger status. Suddenly, I'm a real human being, an individual and not the undifferentiated mass of callers that want something.

In this case, I trained people to say:

Hello, Gary Goodman, Xerox Computer Services for Mr. Smith please; thank you.

That's it? That's all?

No it isn't. There's more, but only if and when you need it.

Sometimes, when you sound authoritative enough, you'll ONLY need this appetizer.

Of course, this raises an intriguing question: How can you sound authoritative?

Let's start with the opposite, how to sound weak, which is probably how you come across, now.

If your tone moves up, as it does when you ask permission, then you sound weak.

Note, normally, we start the call by ASKING for Mr. Smith.

May I speak to Mr. Smith, please?'

This request sends a tonal meta-message that says, "I don't have a right to speak to him. If I did, I wouldn't have to ask!"

So, the answer to not sounding weak, to sounding authoritative, is to tell and not to ask.

Which is to say my voice tone starts HIGH and then goes down the stairs with each word as I announce:

Hello, Gary Goodman, Xerox Computer Services for Mr. Smith please; thank you.

"Hello, Gary Goodman" sounds like I'm saying, "Hi, how are you?"

It's upbeat and cheerful, and then I sounds very businesslike as I say "Xerox Computer Services for Mr. Smith please."

There is no pause between "please" and the words, "thank you."

"Thank you" is said almost under my breath, as a tonal conclusion. I have reached the bottom stair and I am saying, "Now, go get him!"

The pacing of this first line is slow and deliberate. This is sending a meta-message of confidence in myself and in my mission, and it is to permit the listener the chance of processing all of this information the first time he hears it.

Which is very unlikely, no matter how slowly I go. Screeners are so used to their protocol that requires pulling info out like teeth that they are thrown back on their bums when they find no resistance and no tugging is required.

In fact, about 90% of the time you can count on them apologizing!

"I'm sorry, I didn't get that. Would you please repeat that?"

This apology enables us to be magnanimous and to extra slowly say:

"Sure, Gary Goodman, Xerox Computer Services for Mr. Smith please; thank you, again."

Now, the screener is in our communicative debt. He failed to listen and we nicely repeated ourselves. There is a tacit obligation of reciprocity to put us through with no further ado.

But many screeners will go to their next question, but we are way ahead of them. From this point on, we have a suitable scripted reply to every question they could possible have. Each one ends with a directive to bring the sought out executive to the line.

"May I tell him what this is regarding?"

"Certainly, I'm calling at the personal request of our President. Mr. Bill Fello, and I'll be happy to hold, thanks!"

Suddenly, the call is President-to-CEO, corporate officer-to-officer. Note the importance of it, and the implied privacy that it calls for. "Put this call through, right away; it's significant!" is the clear implication of this reply.

And yet, this may still be insufficient to satisfy and engage the cooperation of certain executive, C-suite level screeners.

"Perhaps I can help you?" the screener could offer.

"I wish you could, but I've been asked by Mr. Fello to extend a personal invitation to Mr. Smith and I'll be happy to hold, thanks."

I should disclose that Bill Fello really was President of Xerox Computer Services and I obtained his formal approval to use his name in this manner.

In a notable meeting, he said, "Of course, you can use my name if it will get us meetings. Use-away!"

It really opened doors.

There are several keys to the astonishing success of this campaign. First, it was 100% original. You can't say that about most scripts in the sales world, which are hand-me-downs from quainter era.

There is a threshold question that all of us need to address before we craft any new sales device:

Why is it needed?

The answer must be that we have a recurring blockage that has to be removed. The new screening protocol is needed to get obstructionists out of the way so we can have meaningful and efficient conversations with buyers.

Instead of accepting the sorry state of practice as a functional necessity, we take a fresh look at it and find a way to go over it, around it, under it, or through it.

With my new process, I am breaking out of the typical trap of being at their feet or at their throats. I'm not begging to get through. And I'm not bludgeoning my way through.

I am sounding polite, professional and firm.

Above all, I'm getting a job done with recurring success instead of recurring failure.

This is an odd thing to say, but most salespeople accept their lower status as a matter of fact. "I don't deserve to speak to the CEO of Boeing" is the prevailing sentiment, instead of the opposite.

Also, they whisper to themselves, I have to do exactly what sales traditions would have me do, jot for jot.

This idea, on a tacit, unspoken and unrecognized level, is widespread.

If Meta Selling is saying anything, it is this:

The old ways must give way to the new. And it is up to US to invent these new techniques.

I was hired to help Xerox to sell million dollar packages. The old ways weren't up to the task. As you see in campaign after campaign that I narrate in these pages, Meta Selling breaks the moldy molds of tradition.

The meta-idea I'm asking you to embrace is:

There is a better way!

Meta Sales gambits are new technologies-of-talk. They enable us to multiply our efficiencies and successes, and they simply must be continuously invented and be refined.

Screening innovations help us to prevail in the sale-before-the-sale, as I've said. If we can't sell person #1, the screener, there's no way we'll sell person #2, the actual authorized buyer.

2

How To Be A Mind Reader

Sometimes I'm stunned by how little we know about our prospects. This has to sound odd in a time when we can investigate almost anyone at LinkedIn or Facebook and learn the most obscure details of people's work histories, their education and the experience.

What we don't know, in spite of all of this information, is what is coursing through buyers' minds. If we pitch them, asking for a deal and they say yes, obviously they approve. If they proffer an objection, then they have issues that need to be addressed.

But in between yes and no there is a mysterious realm as big as the red spot on Jupiter.

A few months ago I heard a seller do something brilliant to shed light where there is darkness. It was utterly direct and simple.

He was following-up a proposal, and he asked: "What are you thinking?"

He wasn't trying to force anything. He sounded genuinely curious and interested in hearing any answer that might come forth.

This prompted quality replies. It is an open-ended question, and if you can imagine a huge horse corral, open questions allow prospects to wander almost anywhere they want to go. Of course, there are boundaries at the outer edges, but prospects don't feel them or see them.

No matter what they say in response to, "What are you thinking?" the seller can advance the sales process.

It operates differently than, "Do you like what you see so far?" That forces the listener into a narrow yes-or-no chute. It chafes, and feeling less comfortable, you'll elicit a shallow, reflexive reply.

There's a time for this when you're closing. But if you haven't discussed the merits of a deal yet, and you genuinely don't know what someone is thinking, then by all means, ASK!

You can play the role of the mind reader if they're resisting your inquiry or they're playing the conversation close to the vest.

You can offer this teaser:

"If I'm you, here's what I'm thinking . . ."

I used this one line yesterday. It just popped out. I was on a three-way conference call, trying to put together a deal.

One of the other people was not e helpful by making everything more complicated than it needed to be.

Instead of deferring to him, I did the opposite by meta-communicating.

I said, "If I'm you, here's what I'm thinking: 'Am I looking a gift horse in the mouth? Here's a guy (me) that's bringing (you) a deal with no costs and no risks, right?' "

In truth, that really was the nature of the deal I brought them. We could get started with no out of pocket on their part. Pretty much, I was bringing everything to the party, including the chips and beer.

All they had to do was turn on the ballgame, kick up their feet, and have a good time.

But as Dostoyevsky said, "A man can be in clover. But the clover's not good enough."

They hear a great offer but they're convincing themselves, while you're listening, that there's something wrong with it.

Meta communicating is often getting above the conversation in order to improve it. With the phrase I used, it's opening their eyes to usher in some daylight.

"Yeah, I guess I am looking a gift horse in the mouth" is what I hope they'll think. I'm getting them to question a conclusion they're reached that they were unaware of a moment before.

But what if I'm wrong: The all-knowing, all-seeing Gary missed the mark. What if what I said they're thinking is incorrect?

They'll straighten me out, right? They'll instantly say, "No, you're off-base. HERE'S what I'm thinking."

What a great reply! Now, they're disclosing what's

really holding up the show and I get a chance to deal with the resistance that tipped me off to the need to meta sell to begin with.

I am happy to make a course correction, and then get the deal. There was a comedian who was famous for saying, "You can call me Ray. You can call me Jay. You can call me Johnson."

Call me WRONG: I don't care. If being wrong means I move us in the direction in which I want and need to go, I'll be pleased to be wrong, incessantly.

By using the "If I'm you, here's what I'm thinking" gambit, I'm also doing a little hypnotic suggestion. The technique is actually called mind reading.

We tell people what they're thinking and then if conditions are right, (cue the mood music), they'll adopt our imputation as their own.

"Yes, I'm looking a gift horse in the mouth," they might think. Their next thought is, "It's dumb to look a gift horse in the mouth. Maybe he has a good deal."

They decide their resistance is stupid. That goes down a lot easier than if I accuse them of looking a gift horse in the mouth. If I tell them, we'll have a conflict. If they tell themselves, it is their thought, not mine, and they might chuckle about it. I escape their wrath.

Here's a similar mind-reading meta-communication:

You may be thinking, "It sounds too good to be true," am I right?

There is an unwritten belief in traditional selling: If you uncover and respond to every objection, then a prospect will finally relent and give you the order.

But people might be hesitating not because your deal is too defective.

They might balk because it's too perfect. You could be presenting something that is so airtight it seems unreal. And you can sound too smooth in presenting it to them.

This is a great invitation to Meta Sell. I've used this one, time and again, and it is a masterstroke:

"Sounds too good to be true, doesn't it?"

"Yeah, it does!" they exclaim.

"Well, you're right to think that this offer is not going to last."

Sometimes it's useful to explain briefly why the offer won't last.

Then move seamlessly to a close:

So, I suggest moving forward right away, while we can, Okay?"

People will validate your Meta Selling tactics by using their own meta- communications. For instance, when you're on the mark, addressing their concerns just right, they might chime-in, "You took the words right out of my mouth."

I've heard clients say, "If you're going to save me money, you're speaking my language!"

What prospects are really noting is that it is rare for sellers to be really in sync with buyers. Disconnection and doubt are the typical states of being between parties to a purchase.

In this regard Meta Selling is a real change of pace, and it's relieving and refreshing.

Through much of this book I'm referring to selling that happens one-to-one in person, over the phone, and through email. But you might make group presentations, as I do.

I've conducted hundreds of workshops, seminars and training sessions over the years. Often I've flown into a city for a one-day event at a company.

To get my ideas across and to make for a happy session, I need to put people at ease. I also need to read the tension level of attendees. If they seem scared, or they're wearing looks of apprehension, I'll say with a smile:

"Just a few quick note about how I conduct sessions. I have enough material so I can hold forth all day and not repeat myself. You can sit back and enjoy the show, and I won't call on anybody or put anyone on the spot. Or, we can have more of a free flowing discussion format, addressing your specific situations and needs, if you like. It's up to you. I'm comfortable, either way."

This is also a sort of mind reading. "Gee, I hope he doesn't call on me" and "I don't feel like speaking in front of this group" are two widely held concerns in most gatherings.

I'm saying they can be themselves and we'll still get to where we're going. They're in good hands.

When I offer these words it is amazing how many people smile back at me. You can hear their sighs of relief. And interestingly, the zone of participation becomes very large. Although they thought they wouldn't, most folks actually engage the material and each other and actively contribute to the success of the sessions.

People that felt committed to being deviants, to torpedoing the program with open or furtive hostility, are often defused. Some are actually transformed into friends of the seminar, where they lead discussions into productive areas.

Others, that would have timidly stayed in their shells come out and enjoy the fresh air.

Meta-communicating about how the sessions are conducted allows us to create more pleasant experiences, and more productive ones, too.

The same meta-technique works in every sales medium.

3

Getting People To Call You Back

When I get a call from a number I don't recognize, I let it go to voice mail.

You're probably the same way, because the odds are in favor of that call constituting more of an interruption than a fleeting opportunity.

If no voice mail message is left, I infer I didn't miss anything.

Most legitimate callers will allow their numbers to appear in caller I.D. This that say "number withheld," are typically too flaky to deserve my attention, at all.

If I'm curious, I may take one more baby step just to confirm my suspicions. I'll Google the phone number to see what entries it pulls up.

If I see references to a scam, that totally shuts the door. If it's a survey company calling to get feedback on my recent auto club service, forget about it.

Sometimes, maybe one number in twenty will be someone I recognize with whom I'd like to or need to chat.

There are "spoof numbers" that a computer generates. These show up in caller I.D. and can be only a few digits different than your number. Companies deploy spoofs to get you to think a neighborhood pal or business is trying to reach you. But the call could be from India or some other far away land.

I'm sure you know all about this stuff. I'm bringing it up to make a few points. The first point is it is getting harder all the time to reach people on the first attempt.

And the odds of reaching getting them to answer your unknown number don't significantly improve with more dials. They didn't know you before and they don't know you now.

Jumping ahead for a second, I just love it when amateur sellers leave a voice mail that says, "I've been trying to reach you." Maybe long ago, people felt a duty to reward your efforts to reach them by becoming more reachable.

Maybe they felt a twinge of remorse about not being instantly accessible to everyone.

I don't know about you, but every time I successfully duck a time waster I pat myself on the back. I'm proud of the time I save by being a hermit!

If you feel at all as I do, then so does nearly everyone else. I mean, really, is there anyone out there especially in business that is taking every inbound call aimed at him or her?

If so, how can they have time to do what they really need to do?

Not only will we not reach people on the first or the fifteenth try but if we don't leave a voice mail the chance of them phoning us back is practically zero.

(The odds are a little different for reaching consumers versus businesspeople, but not that much.)

So, to have any chance of eliciting callbacks we need to leave effective voice mails.

What won't work is the standard "tombstone" or business card voice mail:

"Please call Gary Goodman with The Goodman Organization at (818) 970-4279. Thank you."

That might have worked 30 years ago. But today, people need a compelling reason to call you back.

There are two types of voice messages that will do the trick: teasers and pleasers.

Let me share with you a pertinent case study of a wildly successful "teaser" voice mail campaign I constructed, using Meta Selling.

The major complaint I hear from sellers is their voice mail messages fail to elicit returned calls. With one of my consulting clients, they reported receiving a less than 5% voice mail response rate.

They concluded it was literally wasting their breath to leave messages. Dialing the next number on their list in an effort to find a "live" voice with which to chat was a more promising idea.

After implementing my custom crafted techniques, their voice mail response rate soared to 70%, which is nothing short of amazing. 5 out of each 100 responded before I fixed things. 70 out of 100 responded, afterwards.

My client was selling booth space at a job fair that was co-sponsored with the *Los Angeles Times*, a universally known, high-circulation, metropolitan newspaper.

They would leave a typical voice mail, mentioning their company, name and number.

I re-scripted this. I got permission to say they were calling "on behalf of the *LA Times*." Thus vaulted their credibility, instantly.

Then the Meta Sell came in. In trained them to say in an urgent but still pleasant tone, "I'm working on a deadline. Please return my call at this number as soon as you get this . . ."

The phones rang off the hook!

The words, "I'm working on a deadline" were true. They had a limited number of tables to sell to companies at the job fair, and only so much time to do it.

But that phrase also implied that callers were REPORTERS, working on a deadline. This gave the impression that the prospects were being interviewed by the *LA Times*.

"My 15 minutes of fame awaits!" some respondents must have thought, in eager anticipation.

This teaser worked so well that it transformed what had been almost a purely outbound selling function into outbound and inbound. It suddenly became a more stimulating and sales-rich opportunity.

A "pleaser" campaign is a sale-in-short. It is an abbreviated presentation that you leave on voice mail briefly outlining the product or service you're offering along with a testimonial or a recitation of a major benefit in purchasing.

You've heard of "elevator speeches." These are ultra-concise self-introductions of what you do and who benefits from it.

Maybe they last 30 seconds. A pleaser message is like an "elevator sale."

With voice mail you have a minute or more to state your business. If you've crafted your message well, this is enough time to arouse interest.

One of the best types of pleasers is the referral message.

"Hi, this is so and so with such and such and Rick Smith suggested I call you about X."

If Rick is highly regarded, you need to say no more. Your call will be returned.

You can definitely shift the odds of getting people to return your calls if you use intelligence in leaving the best voice mails.

4

Hurricane Gary—
Making Actions Speak Louder

If you sell while on the road, you'll especially appreciate this story.

I was doing an extensive project for a client in Southwest Florida, a region that I came to know pretty well.

For instance, in August, promptly between 4:55 and 5:10 the sky would suddenly darken, and the heavens would burst. An astonishing amount of rain fell within the compass of a few minutes.

And then as suddenly as it started, the storm passed, skies brightened, and the heavy, humid air gave way to something much milder and fragrant.

If you were leaving my client's headquarters during that weather window, you really needed to have an umbrella, or you'd be soaked thoroughly by the time you reached your car, no more than a few hundred feet away.

Even with an umbrella, your shoes could easily get soaked in the puddles that you couldn't avoid. We learned to huddle in the cloisters of the building for the few minutes this meteorological drama took to transact.

But of course, the real weather action came in the form of hurricanes. If you're a roadie, like I was, and that's how you make your living, being in transit, you develop an attitude.

I only earned money when I performed, when I was on-site running classes and seminars and coaching and consulting management. If I was delayed or absent, unlike being an employee, I had no genuine claim on being paid.

So, this made me weather the weather, come what may. On one notable occasion, this meant taking a big risk and really putting myself out to do my professional "act."

A hurricane was off the east coast of Florida when my scheduled landing at Miami's airport was to take place. I was due in at about 9 p.m. so had things gone as planned, that would enable me to catch the last flight over to Fort Myers, arriving about midnight.

At the last minute, my flight was diverted to Orlando. If you know Florida, you know there isn't an efficient way to drive across the state if you don't take Alligator Alley. Hazardous even in bright sunlight, because gators could be loafing on the road, it was infinitely scarier in darkness.

And you can multiply that fear a hundred fold if the weather at night consists of pelting rain and overwhelming wind gusts.

But my motto was like that of the early U.S. postal carriers, "Neither snow nor rain nor heat nor gloom of night stays these couriers from the swift completion of their appointed rounds"

What I decided as I was heading toward Orlando was, come what may, I would arrive at my client's site, ready to perform the next morning.

At the Orlando airport, it was hard finding a taxi. I opted for a limo, and I had to agree to pay a premium to get the driver to pull the all-nighter that it would take to get me to Fort Myers.

The problem was, with all of the blustery weather and non-stop wind and rain, increasing in intensity by the minute, I didn't dare to go to sleep on the way.

Storm conditions and inundated highways were one thing. But stalling out in a gator infested region was another.

At long last, at about 7:15 a.m. I arrived at my hotel. Luckily, I used the same place week after week, so I had a freshly cleaned wardrobe of suits and shirts I could draw from. And my client's building was about two hundred yards from the hotel, easy walking distance.

This enabled me to quickly shave, shower, brush my teeth and pick up a few sweet rolls from the unstaffed buffet that was served each morning.

A little wobbly, but adrenalized, I entered the workplace on time, against all odds.

"When did you get in?" a few people asked. They were aware of the hurricane and my typical route and schedule. Briefly, I explained how the flight was diverted and how I made it across The Alley.

They were duly impressed. They realized I went through heck and high water, literally, to live up to my scheduling commitment.

By simply arriving on time I sent a set of powerful meta-messages.

If I promise to be somewhere, I'll get there.

You're my client, and you're worth going out of my way for.

You can always count on me.

I believe what I'm doing is important enough to justify taking special risks.

I'm responsible.

My absence would have thrown off our schedule, and that's not acceptable to me.

We're going to finish this multi-month program, no matter what.

Researchers refer to visible and audible behavior as "action language." Sometimes this is called nonverbal communication, or body language.

According to some sages in this topical area, we cannot, not communicate. Constantly we're emitting messages, whether we're speaking or not.

Edward T. Hall said, "time talks and space speaks," capturing two nonverbal communication variables.

Being on time or being late is an extremely important source of meaning, depending on one's culture and circumstances.

Braving that hurricane, and still making it to my business engagement on time, spoke volumes about my character.

"This guy is going out of his way for us!" is what they had to be thinking. Considering one of my topics at their site was delivering exceptional customer service, I was walking the walk, not just talking the talk.

There are lots of common phrases for this behavior, including the well worn, "going the extra mile." But note, that is a metaphor for physical conduct, for action language.

If we're walking an extra mile, that's a long way out of our way that we're traversing. That's meaningful, which is to say people make meaning out of that behavior that we're exhibiting.

When I was still fairly new to selling, with only a few years of experience, I was in the car leasing business, in Beverly Hills, California. That place has to be the top of the world when it comes to expensive and exotic rides.

Our sales force, which included me of course, was carefully selected and trained. One of the videos we watched was of legendary football coach, Vince Lombardi, giving an inspiring speech.

Lombardi said: if you're going to a meeting, always arrive 15 minutes early.

This would send a signal of eagerness and integrity. We implicitly make a promise every time we set an appointment, and that promise is to be on time.

Break that promise, and you'll be perceived as unreliable. Live up to it, and you'll be a person "of your word."

He called the 15-minute-early rule, "Lombardi Time."

I lived up to it until I became a college professor. At that time, it was permissible vocation in which to be a little late. I suppose this was a bow to "the absent-minded professor" stereotype that pervades academia.

In fact, though I never personally confirmed this, students were reportedly required to wait for tardy professors to arrive based on the latter's status in the teaching food chain. Ten minutes were allotted for lecturers and assistant professors, and 15 or even 20 minutes for tenured, associate and full professors.

I participated in the largest civilian U.S. Navy management program in history. I was part of a 60-strong, elite cohort that trained 18,000 senior managers in 18 months, and tardiness was strictly and formally forbidden.

We were instructed, "If you're on this team you will not be late, ever. The Navy simply will not tolerate it. We're always, 'on time and on target.'"

Each culture, business, organization, and even family creates its own rituals and rules regarding punctuality. Often, these are not explicitly discussed. They are silently observed.

When someone operates outside of acceptable time tolerances, he is notified. Sometimes this is through frowns, eye contact, checking watches, and other gestures.

Occasionally, rule breakers are explicitly told, you're out of step.

When I was doing a long-term program in Texas, my contact, a senior vice president took me aside. She said:

"I know you're pretty much on your own schedule here, with your trainings. But it looks bad when you leave too early for the day. Like the rest of us, if you can stay until 4:30 or 5:00, that will be better. If this means you take a two-hour lunch, that's okay. The chief idea is to be here at 8:30 and to leave at 5:00, okay?"

I have to admit her admonishment was a little surprising. Clearly, I was in my own business and technically an independent contractor or a vendor, from an accounting standpoint. To me the word, "independent" is the operative term in the phrase, "independent contractor."

As long as I did my work and did it exceedingly well, getting results, I felt I was beyond reproach.

So, on that level, my knee-jerk reaction was defensive. I felt she was out of line.

But discretion prevailed and I went along with her request. It wasn't so bad, except when I had to brave heavier traffic to go back to my suite at the Four Seasons!

She would actually ask me to come aboard as their human resources director, a position they were recruiting for. I demurred, feeling that it would be too constricting, and of course I'd lose all control over my time.

So, as we can see, there are time "heroes" and time "villains." Just the other day I read a book saying that executives that proudly claim to work 60-80 hours a week are grossly exaggerating.

Typically, they're putting in no more than 40 hours, and even that overstates how much actual working time is being dedicated, distraction-free, to being on-task.

Anthropologist Edward T. Hall said our reverence for time is different across cultures. In North America, we're sticklers for punctuality, where this is less of a norm in South American countries, and a certain amount of tardiness is expected and tolerated.

As I've said, you need to put up your antennae to determine what the often unwritten rules are where you're selling, and to whom you're selling. If you're in the dark about it, or confused or just unable to read the tealeaves, then you can ASK.

This is a meta-communication, which we will typically engage in when we're new to a job or location.

To one of our contacts on site, it is good to ask, "When is it customary to take lunch and how long should we take?"

If they respond, "We take 45 minutes," you know that's a rule and you need to abide by it.

But if they say, "About an hour, maybe a little more if you're eating in a restaurant," then it is a standard, not a rule.

Standards involve approximations. For instance, in the driving laws there is language that says you can proceed in fog at a speed that "is safe."

This may be well under the posted limit (if you can read the sign in that soup!) and you need to use reasonable judgment to determine exactly how fast you can go.

In those same conditions, you cannot exceed the posted upper limit, no matter what. That's a rule. It can't be broken, though as a lawyer I can say you'll have a pretty good defense if someone on board has to reach a hospital to deliver a baby.

But you get the point. Meta-communicating by bringing into the open implicit, typically not-discussed rules, can be a smart thing to do.

This pertains to punctuality and to a lot more. But there are some quirks that you should take into account.

One of my professors, Peter F. Drucker, internationally lauded as a management sage, suggested we ask prospects:

How do you like to buy?

The first time I heard him mention this, I was impressed. I thought, why not?

People have buying styles, in the same way that we have preferred selling styles. Generally, I like to speak to buyers in real time, over the phone or face-to-face. This way, I can get real-time feedback, and among other things, instantly shift my techniques and sense when I really have a deal or if someone's stalling is genuine, or reflexive.

If you ask the same folks, how do you like to buy, they could and I expect they would say, by email. Or, they'd quip, "Don't call me, I'll call you!"

In other words, they'll select a medium that actually hinders selling AND buying.

Here is an old fashioned but still pertinent illustration.

Door to door salespeople have always encountered the typical hazards of their trade: locked gates, barking Dobermans, and nosy neighbors.

Also, they have had to respond to posted signs that say, "No Solicitors." In fact, we see the same signs in office buildings.

So, the practical question is, do we still try to sell people that say they don't want to be sold in a certain way?

Here's the counterintuitive answer: We should not only persist after seeing such a sign. We should actually sell these folks, first!

You see, that "No Solicitors" sign is not just a communication, sending the obvious message you and I know it is sending.

It is also meta-communicating. That meta-message is, "We have so little sales resistance that we bought and posted this sign to prevent us from buying everything that's offered!"

They're pushovers! Easy-peasy-lemon-squeezy buyers— that's what they're branding themselves with those words, "No Solicitors."

And by extrapolation, they're also saying that sign does deter most sellers that see it. Thus the occupants have less sales resistance because they're unpracticed in using it. Their "no-muscles" have atrophied, leaving them defenseless to any and all offers.

Their action, by sign posting, speaks louder than their words, which is the theme of this section.

Make sure to choose your actions carefully for the meanings they convey, electing the ones that help your cause, instead of hindering it.

5

What Does "Responsibly Sourced" Mean?

The other day I was shopping for a couple of steaks at one of my local grocery stores.

For a long time, this chain was part of Safeway, which of all large grocers has boasted the best beef, overall, of any. I know this, not only because it has passed my own informal comparative tastes tests, but also because I am a Safeway School graduate.

I hope you're smiling, because this is a peculiar distinction that I have never put on my resume. In the company of 5 earned college degrees, it might have appeared to be an odd or silly distinction.

But in regard to lifetime cash value, my "diploma" from that 2-week, paid training program has saved me tens of thousands of dollars. Which puts it ahead of the value some poor souls say they have derived from their actual degrees.

Of course, I worked for Safeway, and their school was a program all new retail clerks, stocking folks and cashiers had to navigate. Mere grocery baggers, one of whom I had been before moving up to clerk-hood, were not invited to attend.

Sandwiched into the course were solid tips about purchasing one's own provisions. We were told about the distinctions between store brands and costlier famous brands that are advertised like crazy. This alerted us to the all-important idea that in many, not all, but many product lines, buying the grocery company's own labeled fare was significantly cheaper and as good tasting as the nationally advertised competitors.

The cool thing about my grocery education, as well as the training I received in the car business, and at my insurance clients' site, is that I emerged from these experiences as a far smarter consumer than "civilians" that had never enlisted in these industries.

I received meta-knowledge, insider savvy about where and how the biggest profits are made. This put me into "the know" about how to save big, as well.

So, as I was buying my steaks, another gentleman was being served. Noticing a sign in the meat case, he chortled to the butcher, "What does 'responsibly sourced' mean?"

The butcher simply ignored the question, or may have furtively winced and carried on to finish the order.

I suppressed a grin of my own, because I was impressed that the consumer (1) Noticed the meta-message to begin with; (2) He was "talking-back" to it; and (3) So few people do this.

Consider the fact that this grocery chain has introduced "talking" signs that not only say "choice" or "prime," conveying the physical and taste characteristics of the meat.

They have also introduced rhetoric of morality, of "goodness," of virtue into the dialogue. So, suddenly, readers have to take into account the diligence or the discretion with which the cattle were handled.

I wonder what irresponsibly sourced would mean. Would this be any old cow that bandits may have purloined (or would that be, sirloined)?

Adding to the mystery is this definition offered at Google:

> *"Sometimes referred to as supply chain responsibility environmental and social factors into account when managing their relationship with suppliers responsible sourcing is a voluntary commitment made by companies to take environmental and social factors into account when managing their relationship with suppliers."*

When it comes to fish, I suppose the idea is clearer. Responsibly sourced might mean you haven't fished out the Caspian Sea so much that you have completely eliminated its famous stocks of sturgeon, denying the 1% their fair share of caviar.

This rhetoric is a throwback to when I was in my Ph.D. program at USC. A fellow student worked at a museum's restaurant, in which he became a partial owner.

Ian, who was a wonderful but overwhelming presence there, had the gift of gab and he wanted more than anything to discuss the food he was serving. He would interrupt any bites he could to determine if they were tasty, and then not so subtly monitor the satisfaction patrons experienced as they licked their plates clean.

The oddball TV series "Portlandia," parodied this sort of behavior, perfectly. (Disclosure: descriptive license taken.)

A young couple is gazing (should I say grazing) at the menu when the server asks what they'd like. Everything is so responsibly sourced, I guess, that they're able to order a chicken by its proper name.

"We're thinking of having Penelope, but we have just a few questions about her."

Well, the back and forth goes on and on until the server invites the couple to inspect the farm where Penelope was raised. A cult runs the place, and the couple falls in with them. Finally, they extricate themselves, returning to the restaurant, perhaps weeks or months later.

The same server asks them, "Have you decided?"

"We're not going to have Penelope, after all," they say. "What can you tell us about Fred?"

So, where are we going with this?

Do I have too much time on my hands that I'm wasting in deconstructing meat case language?

No, there is a serious point. There is a movement afoot in sales and marketing to affiliate one's companies and products with trendy environmental and social causes.

One of the first companies to conspicuously do this is Newman's Own. Here's their story, succinctly recited at the company's web site:

"Newman's Own Foundation celebrates 35 years of giving. Thanks to our founder, Paul Newman, who started Newman's Own in 1982 with a single salad dressing and decided to donate 100% of the profits to charity. We continue his legacy today and recently reached a milestone of $530 million in donations, helping thousands of charities and millions of people around the world."

Innumerable companies are doing a version of this "giving back" to the community. So, the meta-message to buyers of Newman's dressing is if you purchase our brand, you're nourishing yourself and society, as well.

Patagonia, the clothing and equipment manufacturer, has done something similar. They got their start by using recycled and repurposed materials in constructing their stock in trade. This story is told well, in founder Yvon Chouinard's book, *Let My People Go Surfing*.

A mountaineer, Chouinard invented what he calls, "clean climbing." It is a way of leaving a mountain's climbing surface in much the same shape in which you found it, as pristine as possible. His gear is made to facilitate this outcome.

Thus, when you buy Newman or Patagonia, you're buying the feeling that you're not selfishly indulging. You're giving while you're getting.

My question is this: Are we heading into a time when all companies will feel obliged to "tithe" in this way? Must you have a meta-story that involves benevolent heroics to cultivate and capture a loyal fan base?

In both cases, Newman's Own and Patagonia, their offerings are not cheap. "Do-gooding " does not mean cost cutting. In fact, it is usually the reverse.

You can justify higher prices because you're subsidizing nonprofit motivations with for-profit methods.

But it doesn't always work this way, or this seamlessly.

Eventuating in a famous Supreme Court case, Hobby Lobby mixes the Christian faith of its owners with the sale of its goods. It isn't unusual to enter a store to buy a picture frame that has a cardboard or paper insert with a scriptural passage printed on it.

It should be noted that Hobby Lobby's prices are frequently lower than its competitors' prices. This belies what I said above about Newman's and Patagonia.

As a seller these days, do you also need a parallel nonprofit goal to accompany your obviously for-profit one?

Must your goods and services not only be efficient and economically valuable, but are we in a purchasing milieu in which they must also convey or arouse a sense of received or donated virtue?

At the beginning of my seminars for businesses and other organizations I've found it is helpful to tell my professional story.

Sometimes, I'll go as far back as to say I used to marvel at my Dad's selling abilities and methods. I go on to say I worked my way in sales and sales management through college and grad schools, rising in the ranks as I went along.

I've noticed, when I leave these Abe Lincoln, why I walked 10 miles to in the snow get to school, details out of my self-introduction, people react very differently to me and to my material.

They're more open, more communicative, and friendlier when they feel I earned my right to speak to them "the good-old fashioned hard way."

Strictly speaking, when they subscribe to a seminar or to my extended corporate training, they're signing on for information and techniques.

Who I am can be just as pertinent to them as what I'm saying.

So, Gary-the-Myth, the back-story, the narrative of how we came together, these details contain some of the "virtues" they're buying.

Without them, I'm not as credible, or as persuasive, or as successful.

And my efforts to communicate my history aren't cynical attempts to court approval. They meta-communicate that on a financial level the tuition being paid for my classes is partly a set-off against the huge investments I made in receiving my own academic and corporate education.

I forwent lots of earnings while I was in school, and I paid hundreds of thousands in tuition, out of pocket, when assessed at current valuations.

Thus, you're buying a multi-million-dollar education (mine!) when you're buying me.

By golly, you're responsibly sourcing!

As a seller you should determine how much your back-story about yourself and your company you should tap.

It can make a huge difference in your professional sustainability!

6

What's It Going To Be: Yes, No or Maybe?

There is a scene in the movie, "Pleasantville," a throwback to the 1950's, in which a car pulls into a "service" station and team of eager, crisply uniformed guys leap out of nowhere to pump the fuel, clean the windshield, check the tire pressure, and read the oil dip stick.

The scene is funny precisely because it is such an anachronism. "Full service" stations, where they exist, are likely to charge you an extra dollar per gallon merely to pump your gas. Mostly, they're gone from the scene.

About the same time, there was an unwritten rule of etiquette that said if you leave a phone message for someone, that person is duty-bound to return your call. It was labeled, a "common courtesy," and it was widely observed, especially in business.

If someone was calling you, long-distance, you made a special effort to be at your phone to accept the outreach because faraway calls cost substantially more than local ones.

Today, those rules have pretty much gone by the wayside, except in certain circles. Until fairly recently, if I phoned someone in a university, a fellow professor or an administrator at another campus, there was a 75% or better chance I'd receive a prompt reply.

To give you a sense of how the rules have changed, at UCLA, where I have taught for 20 years, if I leave a phone message or send an email chances are that I will be ignored 90% of the time. I'm treated like a stranger, or like a mere supplicant, though I have a long a successful track record.

(Berkeley, where I have taught for 11 years, is a different story, happily. It may take a few days, but my communications are heard and reciprocated.)

Making real-time contact with sales prospects has never been harder. And it's easy to understand why.

Unless I recognize the caller I.D. I don't answer my phone. Moreover, I set my device to "silent mode" most of the time, unless I'm expecting an urgent contact.

I'm one of the millions of hard-to reach people, and being inaccessible serves me quite well. Most unrecognizable inbounds are intruders of various types, with no claim to my immediate attention.

And I abide by the idea that if someone calls and it is important, they'll leave a voice mail that I can listen to later and then respond, if needed.

This is essential if I want to get anything of importance done. There is an entire book devoted to this topic, titled *Deep Work*, which pretty much affirms this and other defensive fortress maneuvers.

To be as effective as we can be requires us to immerse ourselves. We simply cannot afford to be rousted from our depths to be pitched or to be bothered.

I'm fairly certain you feel the same way. If you're a serious person, or even an unserious one with responsibilities, you have to take the reins of your own time. If you cede your attention to every momentary distraction, you'll pay a heavy and unacceptable price.

I've taken some pains to unearth these feelings because buyers are just like us. They simply don't want to be bothered.

Yet getting their attention is our specific job.

I remember making calls to households for Time-Life books. My first shift was part-time, from 6 p.m. to 9 p.m.

Every night, one or two people would bristle: "Why must you people call at the dinner hour?"

The rudely right reply none of us dared to utter was:

We phone at dinnertime because that's when you're at home!

There were some other reasons. "Dinnertime" could reasonably span 4 p.m. to 9 p.m. or later. If we avoided everyone's dinnertime we'd never make a single call.

Infamous bank robber Willie Sutton was asked why he robbed banks: "Because that's where the money is," he replied.

I'm saying if you dare to communicate anything to anyone at anytime you are daring to interrupt his or her activity.

Selling is an interruption, always, because there is never a time when someone is not doing something else!

I know, these things should go without saying, and they normally do. But because they remain tacit, we trip ourselves on them.

We need to meta-communicate to ourselves that it is normal and permissible to interrupt people to sell them something. Our products deserve their attention to a greater degree than the trivial things they were doing when we reached out to them.

We can even say it, and maybe we should, more often.

Imagine phoning someone who says, "I'm kind of doing something right now."

Kind of doing something?

That's a weak excuse.

Why not reply, "Well I appreciate that and I'll make it brief." Then, continue with your presentation as if the interruption never occurred.

If we are genuinely offering something that will improve that person's life or career we have every right to try to accomplish this goal, correct?

How else are they going to learn about what we're offering?

In screenplays there is a term for when two protagonists unexpectedly come into each other's lives. It is termed, "Meeting Cute."

They both try to grab a taxi in a thunderstorm at the same time and get tangled up in the process. Their eyes lock-and-glaze. There's electricity.

They've "met cute."

Buyers love to meet cute. Somehow, cosmic forces bring you together with them and they fall madly in business with you.

That practically never happens, which is why it's so much fun seeing the romantic version being portrayed on the screen.

What really happens is a seller makes a move on a buyer, introducing himself and pitching a deal.

To become a successful seller you have to be okay with taking the lead, crossing the dance floor, convincing the clumsy they have some smooth moves in them.

There is an expression in selling that comes to mind:

People don't like to be sold, but they love to own.

Meaning, they are going to love your products and services after they have committed to them and they are using them, gaining advantages and satisfactions from doing so.

They don't know this. In fact, they're convinced that it will be the opposite, until they are proud owners.

It's a little like having kids. It may not seem like a good proposition, with the diapers and crying and changes they'll make in what used to be your lifestyle.

But then it happens. They're ready to be driven home from the hospital. They're yours!

And everything you thought you'd feel is wrong. Soon, the time will come when you can't remember life with out them, and you don't want to.

I've always marveled at how buyers come to think about employing me. They might be skeptical at first, but then we get underway and we're achieving success, together.

Someone they know asks, "How did you two meet?"

There's a pause, and we realize that I cold-called them. I sold them out of the blue. We were complete strangers, and they took a leap of faith.

But here we are, possibly months or even years down the road, and we realize it doesn't really matter how they bought, as long as they bought.

(Unless I'm teaching cold-calling techniques, where it becomes genuinely pertinent, and even helpful to the program's credibility.)

So, you have every right to intrude, to say pay attention to me and pay heed to my offer. And, once you have pitched someone, you have a right to be informed of his or her decision to move forward, or to pass.

This is one place where I still believe buyers have an obligation to respond, to communicate. Let's say you've gone to the trouble of making a sales presentation and sending out collateral material.

I believe there is an unwritten rule that says your prospects should then tell you where your proposed deal stands.

Is it still pending? Has there been a decision? What is it? Do you need to do anything on top of what you've already done to seal the deal?

Did you leave out something pertinent?

They should tell you, and promptly. I just said, "should," didn't I?

There's a tipoff in that. I'm idealizing when I speak about "should be." That's probably not the way things work.

Back to my college-communication example, where I can have a long-term relationship with them and still be ignored. Functionaries in most companies are as bad at responding, or are worse.

What can you do? I meta-communicate.

I'll leave voice mails and send emails saying I'm following-up and would they kindly:

"Get in touch right away, by voice, text or email and indicate whether the proposed deal is a yes, no, or a maybe. Thank you very much."

This works very well. Some will still string you along, and say they're still considering your offer when there isn't any genuine interest, or there's no forward momentum toward a deal.

But this does give me a few firm, nos. To me, they are second-best responses.

Here is the order I like: (1) Yes (2) No (3) Maybe (4) Silence.

Silence is the killer. It offers no meaningful feedback. And I find it contemptuous of the entire process.

I pitched a CPA firm on joining forces to sell a tax debt resolution service fashioned after my experience as an attorney and salesperson. I felt it was a wonderful opportunity, so I reached out.

We met in person, somewhat oddly at an area Starbucks, and not in his office. He said he didn't want his people overhearing our conversation. Later, I'd invest some time there, casually monitoring sales efforts, and I'd determine why he was reluctant.

He and his staff were crammed into a shoebox.

Each time I'd visit, I couldn't wait to breathe fresh air and put space between us. It was like an aversion reaction.

Anyway, I thought we had the outline of a deal and proposed a start date. Silence ensued. Weeks passed. No calls or emails were made back to me.

Finally, he got in touch, noting that he had some family troubles. Okay, I cut him some slack and it seemed we were back on track, with a start date approaching.

Then the same prolonged silence ensued.

Silence is its own meta-message. We interpret it various ways. I was interpreting his to say, he is a flake who cannot be trusted.

Working against my strong instinct to cut explicitly him loose, I counseled myself that he could simply not be ready. In his rude way, he was signaling this lack of readiness.

It didn't mean my idea was a bad one. It would keep, I could wait, I told myself.

Finally, we had a flurry of focused activity and a start date was approaching. But then it was my turn to stall because I had taken on an important project that I wanted to complete with distinction, free from distraction.

He grew agitated that I didn't immediately return one of his emails that really needed no acknowledgment.

"I expect you to tell me you promptly that you have received my emails," he meta-communicated in yet another email.

By that time, it had become clear to me that he had two sets of communication rules, one for him and one for me. That wasn't going to work.

And neither was I, at least with him.

So, looking back, I should have followed up and insisted on receiving a yes-no-maybe update from him. I could have explicitly said, as he would later indicate: "Silence is not an option."

From time to time, I break my own rules for selling. This is to test their continuing relevance. Maybe something has changed, I tell myself. Let's find out . . .

In his case, I offered far more patience than I normally do. I supposed I could have cased that in for some sort of benefit with him, but I couldn't tolerate his work style or workplace.

I did get a deal from a contact in Northern California who would later say, as I left her business for the last time on the way to the Sacramento airport, "Thank you for your persistence!"

What a nice acknowledgment she made. I put up with a number of delays before delivering what turned out to be a very successful training program.

But she should have known, by explicitly appreciating my persistence, she would receive more of the same in the future.

I pitched a follow-up program, about a year later. And I followed-up, which is what a persistent person does.

But alas, I didn't get that deal.

I wish she had meta-communicated at an earlier point:

"I know I thanked you for your persistence, before. And I meant it. But this time, there's no use in persisting. We're not buying."

Does this sound too explicit? Is it verging on cruelty? It's certainly blunt and to the point.

But it would have saved me a lot of time, and therefore money. And it would have spared her time and energy, along with that of her assistants and receptionists that helped her to dodge my calls.

What prospects and non-buyers don't appreciate is the fact that being indirect with sellers, going into radio-silence, stalling us, and using other avoidance tactics introduces added costs into the sales process.

These costs are going to be reflected in higher prices, if not to them, then to the next person in line that does choose to buy. Costs end up spiraling for everyone, resulting in inflation and higher prices.

Even if you escape paying and your neighbor does instead, that is an added cost to the community. We're all made inefficient and poorer for your wasting of my time!

I've actually gone so far as to say this to various prospects. I've meta-communicated that avoiding a sales process isn't as free as it seems, unless you become transparent and signal your true reactions to proposals and your true circumstances and intentions.

So, what's it going to be: Yes, no, or maybe?

7

From Those Wonderful Folks That Gave You Pearl Harbor!

Jerry Della Femina is a legendary advertising guy, a creative type that would have fit perfectly into the TV show, "Mad Men."

Known for his off the wall ad themes, he was the genius behind such starker's as this pithy catch phrase for a Japanese automaker:

From Those Wonderful Folks That Gave You Pearl Harbor!

He went on to author a book with this grabber as his title.

I have to say I just love this stuff. The outrageous eye-catching motto is something I relish. During college, I even pitched myself for a copywriting job at a leading ad agency, having grown up in the ad business, watching my dad have loads of professional fun.

Dad, for instance, had clients like the rock group, "The Doors." He posed for photos with Jim Morrison and the rest of the guys. As a joke, artists added some long hair to his pics, making Dad seem like just another Door, or maybe an odd hinge.

During that era, maybe a little later, there was an ad that caught my eye that ran for General Tires.

Boldly, the headline in print, billboards, TV and radio declared:

Sooner or Later, You'll Own Generals.

Talk about meta-selling! The geniuses behind this assertion were appealing to an extremely powerful persuasive ploy, an appeal to inevitability.

In Sci-Fi movies, aliens croak something similar:

Resistance is futile! Surrender earthlings!

Imagine conversing with someone you just met who tells you, flat-out, "Say yes now, and save us both some time."

That would be a pretty extraordinary meta-communication, correct?

That's exactly the seed that General Tire was planting. Here's the logic.

If you're going to buy anyway, why not buy sooner than later? If buying is a good idea, wouldn't it be advantageous to elongate the receipt of benefits starting right now?

Conversely, why would you want to delay the advantages owning this item will confer?

I've used this very appeal when selling six-figure consulting projects.

Prospects look stupefied when I lay this technique on them.

By using this idea I'm turning the tables. Essentially, I'm challenging them to tell me why they would delay.

"Why wouldn't you buy, and the sooner the better?"

I admit, this can sound nasty and snarky, almost like I'm taunting them. So, it's best to add an innocent, soft delivery of your words to make it effective, but friendly.

The argument to inevitability is a two-edged sword. Its strength is that it is definite, conclusive, and supremely confident.

That's also its potential weakness because seeming certain can rile certain people.

"You're going to go clean your room!"

"You can't make me!"

The "you're going to" can elicit almost a reflexively defensive, "no I'm not."

Generally, we resist being told what to do and when we're going to do, but General Tire broke that rule.

And there's almost a winking at the consumer of this message, that "You'll own Generals" conveys along with the content.

This is similar to the example I gave in another segment of this book, about of one of my best-selling book titles: *You Can Sell Anything By Telephone!*

The meta-messages that accompany this title are, "Don't tell me you can't, because you can!" and "Yeah, you can even sell that, too!"

There's almost a playful fighting tension in the phrase itself. Again consider Della Femina's:

From Those Wonderful Folks That Gave You Pearl Harbor!

The absolutely outrageous nature of this headline is a force of nature. Treating the introduction of a car from your "worst enemy" as a Coming Attraction, as you'd see in a movie theater, was way off the charts.

But it works!

If you're like me, someone that loves to craft ditties like this one, you can't help but wonder, where do these lines come from?

Sometimes, I think they come to the fore when we're relaxed and having fun. I know my mind plays with the words it sees, and usually I'm along for the ride.

For instance, I wanted to write a book that would help people to deal effectively with their debts. Having experience in credit card, student loan, and tax debt resolution, I knew my topic.

And my angle was different than preaching restraint in spending, cutting up your credit cards, and the conventional wisdom on the subject.

But I couldn't get past the boring sound of "How To Get Out Of Debt," which is a sleep-inducing title.

That phrase even made my eyes glaze over, though it was a pretty accurate description of the content I expected to present.

Then, it hit me. People don't just want to lower their debts or gradually and painfully retire them.

They want to eliminate them. They want to run away from them and from the debt collectors that are hot on their heels.

They want to pay NOTHING if they can get away with it.

THEY WANT TO STIFF THEIR CREDITORS, COMPLETELY!

That's where my title, *Stiff Them!* came from. The subtitle followed easily and naturally: How To Pay Zero Dollars, etc.

Freud came up with a theory of consciousness that contains three levels, the Id, the Ego, and the Superego. The Id is the deepest level, almost a reptilian brain, filled with who-knows-what, a swamp of drives and symbols and mysteries.

At the Superego level, the personality we present to the world, we typically abide by all social conventions. Paying one's bills is a norm, a customary practice, and seeming to do this is important to the Superego, which is vitally aware of how we are perceived by others.

On an Ego level, we want to see ourselves as responsible for our actions. We also want to believe that we are in charge of our own lives. Paying back our debts is consistent with maintaining our image of ourselves contained in our Egos.

But on that deepest of levels, the Id, we're a floating mass of hot magma. If we can't get our way, when we're frustrated or feel threatened, when we, and our loved ones, are at risk we erupt. Right and wrong give way to Survival, whatever it takes.

That's where I'm reaching people with *Stiff Them!*

Yeah, those folks gave us Pearl Harbor, the worst tragedy in American history. But they make a really good car!

Here are my first words in the book, *Stiff Them!:*

We all want to do the right thing.

That's the prim and proper Superego speaking. That's the hope, the aspiration, the shined shoes we step into the world of society, with.

But sometimes, WE CAN'T! And dang it, we can't be expected to pay for our mistakes, forever.

Thus, the Id intones, through the primal, sulfuric mist, Stiff Them!

As a communication theorist I've often thought the most effective language we can use with sales prospects and customers is the language they use when they speak to themselves. Matching these thoughts and the feelings that accompany them is the quickest path to a yes.

For example, I came up with this close, which as you know is a strategic way to win approval for your offer:

Sounds good, doesn't it?

This is a meta-close because it gets the prospect to comment, affirmatively, about the pitch I've just made. It also echoes what we tell ourselves, silently, as we hear something appealing, "That sounds good."

Dinner is on the stove or cookies baking in the oven and we whisper to ourselves, "That smells good!"

One of the keys to developing these meta-communications is to meta-communicate with oneself.

Ask yourself: What do I REALLY want to say, here?

What phrase or motto or headline cuts to the chase?

Sometimes, the answers come to us in a pique of frustration.

When I coach people I can be relentless in reshaping their messages until they are just right. Typically, they're too long. They wander. They veer off-topic. They include peripheral information.

So, I'll demand, "Make it shorter. Cut it in half." At first, they'll balk, but then they'll follow orders, which cuts out some fluff.

"Say this another way. Cut to the chase. Why are you saying you're so good?"

It was this process that I put myself through that eventuated in that great line I coined for my own company, mentioned in another section:

What we do works!™

When all is said and done, leaving aside all of the specific features and benefits of my processes and ideas, what are we left with?

Distilled to its essential elements, I'm saying we're effective. But there's more. That's about us.

It has worked for others and it will therefore work for you. That's the key.

The meta-message, unspoken but still palpable, is:

It's safe to approve this contract and to undertake the program because you'll get the results I'm promising.

There is an implied guarantee when I say: What we do works!™

Guarantees are exceedingly powerful meta-messages that say you can buy with confidence. (And, if you feel you made a mistake, you can undo it.)

This is worth understanding in depth.

Why do people hesitate to buy? Maybe they haven't been convinced they'll receive sufficient value to offset the purchase price. This results from inadequately understanding the benefits they'll receive from owning.

But they also hesitate because they're afraid they'll make a mistake. And they're concerned that if they do make a mistake it will be irreversible. They'll lose money, and if their loss is conspicuous, they'll be subjected to shame or punishment.

A guarantee gets people over these concerns. It says, and you can communicate it this way if you like:

You can't make a mistake. We guarantee (your satisfaction) or (our products will perform exactly as specified.)

You can oversell a guarantee, to your detriment. If you push on the idea that buyers can undo deals, they'll undo deals!

We saw this at Time-Life. We were using a 10-day trial to get our books into prospects' hands. "Try it for 10-days," was the basic pitch.

But if we added, "You can always return it, with no obligation, if you don't like it" we got into trouble. Our returns would soar, which cost the company a lot of money.

So we ended up with this almost perfect compromise:

"Try it for ten days, without obligation. If it isn't everything I've said, it can be returned, but we know you'll want to keep it, Okay?"

There is a considerable amount of research in communication theory about "primacy-versus-recency." Which is more persuasive, the first message people hear or the last one they hear?

Note in the trial language we started with, "Try it for ten days, without obligation." That's the first message the prospect hears, saying you have the power to send the book back.

But the last message is, "But we know you'll want to keep it, Okay?"

At Time-Life, we found it was the last message that was most persuasive. If we ended on a positive note, people bought the book after the ten-day trial.

But if we closed with this phrase, we ended up in the loss column:

"So, let's get this out to you on the 10-day trial, and if you don't like it for any reason, simply send it back, Okay?"

To really appreciate the impact, consider this. When we're selling we're also instructing buyers in how to behave. Look at the final words in the respective Time-Life closes:

". . . but we know you'll want to keep it, Okay?"

". . . simply send it back, Okay?"

In the first, we say, keep it, Okay? In the second we say, send it back, Okay?

We found prospects did what we instructed them to do with our final words.

Regarding communication theory, recency won over primacy.

As a final note, I should say guarantees are exceedingly powerful in helping us to close deals. I cover this topic in detail in my course and book, *Dr Gary S. Goodman's 77 Best Practices in Negotiation*.

I point out there are two kinds of guarantees, and you should be aware of them. They are subjective and objective.

If I close you with the following one, it is a subjective guarantee: If for any reason you don't like it, simply return it for a full refund.

The "for any reason" says you could wake up on the wrong side of the bed and undo the deal for that or any old reason. In fact, you don't need a reason, or an excuse, as such.

An objective guarantee is what I offer to some of my call center clients. I tell them, if they purchase my training and follow my instructions, their calls will become 20-30% shorter.

If they stay the same length or get longer, all things being equal, my clients don't have to continue with my program. We take a pre-program measurement of average call length, so we know exactly how much call length we have or have not reduced.

There are some other particulars involved, but my guarantee is an objective one.

I prefer objective guarantees for numerous reasons. They are easily monitored, measured, and managed. They don't depend on the whims and changing tastes of buyers or sellers to uphold.

In a word, they're fair.

And because they are spelled out in mutually understandable terms, they are themselves a meta-language for interpreting success and failure.

I love the transparency, and at times, even outrageous humor that meta-selling can tap.

And for this we can thank those wonderful folks that gave you this book: my publishers!

8

Should You Dress For Success Or Look Good?

May I tell you about my career in the vacuum cleaner business? Don't worry; it won't take long.

That career lasted all of one day. But I'm getting ahead of myself.

I was 18, and I answered an ad in the newspaper. Showing up at the Electrolux dealership in Westwood, California, I had no clue about the adventure that awaited me.

I chatted with the amiable manager and looked around at the poorly lit display. Clearly, they were scrimping on electricity. From the outside, the place had the vacant look of someone that had hit the snooze button.

I can say the inside was well vacuumed, if nothing else. Spotless carpet, it was, but you'd expect that.

I was told I would do a ride-along with Jimmy, an incongruously peppy name for a fellow that had been selling for a half-century.

"Now, what you need to remember, GARY, is not to say a word! This is an observation day. Watch what Jimmy does, because he's our top salesman."

That sounded fine with me, but from the look of Jimmy, I was not encouraged.

If you consult the dictionary you'll find this word: Frumpy. It means out of fashion and old. Jimmy's attire was worse.

It came closer to being defined as tattered, frayed, timeworn, and threadbare.

If it weren't for his white shirt and necktie, Jimmy could have been mistaken for being a bum.

"How am I going to learn anything from this guy?" I wondered.

"Walk with me out to my car," he grumbled in a way that said I didn't impress him, either.

Two Cadillacs and a beaten up station wagon were parked together.

He opened the trunk of the bight red Caddy and extracted an Electrolux machine with hose attached.

"We're not taking this car," he smiled. Heading toward the wagon, he added, "We're taking that one."

Suddenly, my mind recalculated. This guy is an old, frumpy-and-then-some salesman who dresses in tatters and he owns this hot red Cadillac?

The one with spotless, white tuck and roll upholstery?

Impossible, yet there were two of these rides parked out back. The other one, slightly less flashy, but larger, must have been the manager's.

My head was spinning. These guys were making more money than I ever imagined!

We drove to the nice Rancho Park area of homes.

"We're going to work this street," he said flatly.

"Want me to carry that?" I asked, eager to do something to help this frail guy out.

"No way!" he answered.

We went door to door offering a free cleaning of the living room carpet, easily the biggest area in each house.

Homemakers would predictably reply, "Why I just vacuumed, and it's already clean."

"May I very quickly do it again to see if there's anything your machine missed?" my new partner asked, sweetly.

"Well, I suppose there's no harm in that!" would be the reply, also on cue.

Then the drama began. "Did you clean back here?" he asked.

"Oh, yes, of course?"

"May I move the couch a tad to also get back here?" he inquired.

"Please do."

After about fifteen minutes he shut off the machine and went into his set-up.

"Okay, so we started with your cleaned carpet that your current machine already took care of. By the way, how old is it, again?"

"I don't know, maybe 5 years old?"

"Your 5 year old machine," he trailed off, shaking his head.

Then, deftly detaching the bag from the machine, he went to the middle of the room and declared, "Then this bag should be empty, right?"

And with the flourish of a magician, he turned it up-side down, producing a mountain of filth.

"Oh, my!" the homemaker gasped.

At this point, a crucial silence ensued during which Jimmy let the embarrassment and shame well up in the prospect. I was ashamed for her, and I just had to help her out, even if it meant breaking my vow of silence.

About to interject something stupid, to help her to save face, the wily coyote stared me down and continued his talk.

"Just look at that filth your old machine is leaving behind. And you and your family are breathing that and totally unaware. And you are working to keep it clean but can't make it so, not with that old vacuum!"

"You don't want to live with this dirt, do you?"

At this point, the homemaker was close to tears.

"No worries, I'll take it off your hands and we'll give you full credit on this new Electrolux."

Then he started writing up the order.

I expected Rod Serling from "The Twilight Zone" to stroll in and soberly recite an epilogue.

"Here we have a typical homemaker who has been sharing her typical suburban home with a silent enemy, filth. Thought to be a trusted pal, her old faithful vacuum cleaner has been quietly, but steadily betraying her. But-for her knight with shining aluminum, disguised as he was in rags and tatters, she would have never emerged from this domestic nightmare. A sales story with a twist, from The Twilight Zone."

I have to emphasize the fact that from beginning to end, this pathetic, pitiful presence known as Jimmy, was a masterful illusionist. He came across exactly as he needed to come across for the sole purpose of selling more vacuums than anyone else in the region.

Returning to the shop, he figured I had seen enough to determine if I could make a go of it.

But he asked me anyway, "What do you think?"

Before I could reply he felt duty bound to teach me a lesson. Suddenly, he sounded very crisp and professional, you might say tutorial and sophisticated.

"You were about to say something at that sale, weren't you? Big mistake, it would have screwed-up the whole thing. Everything is carefully planned, and you can't add anything or leave anything out."

I wanted to say, "Yeah, but you made her cry! You didn't have to do that."

Yes, he did. It was all part of the drama, and even Aristotle, in his work of genius, "The Poetics," said the play must arouse "pity and fear for the proper purgation of the emotions."

From a dramatic standpoint, she wasn't crying, she was purging her emotions. It was necessary for her to assert she was a wonderful homemaker. She cleaned, every day.

But there was proof she was failing. Piled high, as Mt. Everest on her living room rug was all the evidence needed to see the disgrace.

She lost face, but this salesman would help her to quickly restore it.

She could easily buy her way out of the shame, while making her tears, happy ones.

The arc of the sale, a subject you won't find being discussed in most sales books, involves a motivated sequence of persuasion. Change that sequence, or if you will, the script, and the inevitable conclusion, the proper purgation of the emotions, doesn't happen.

"Are you wondering why we didn't take the Cadillac?" my partner asked.

"We didn't take it because they won't buy if they think you're rich or too well-off. I live in a gated community. I play golf every afternoon. I earn more than they do, and live far better. But I can't show it or it will all go away."

I felt like blurting out, "Yeah, but you look like a bum! I can't dress like that!"

But I remained silent, nodded my head, and meekly thanked him and the manager and made it out the door.

I had studied drama at one of the most renowned high schools on the planet. Yet I wasn't right for this role.

You've heard of Head & Shoulders shampoo, haven't you? Here we had a guy that would have ADDED dandruff to his shoulders if he thought it would earn him an additional sale.

I didn't want to be pathetic. I wanted to be respected, dignified!

I related better to one of the characters in the play and movie, "The Producers." Speaking of wealth and the look of it, he beamed, "If you've got it, FLAUNT IT!"

Not, if you've got it, hide it. What's the value of getting it if you can't display it?

But that was the naïve thinking of the18 year-old Gary.

Now, I appreciate so many things about my career-day in the vacuum cleaner business.

For one thing, "dressing for success" is not about looking sharp and well tailored.

It is about looking appropriate.

Down to the last frayed thread, Jimmy looked the part of a humble vacuum seller. His outfitting said, "Hey, there's not that much profit in these machines," when in truth, the margins were huge.

Not one thing, not a gold pinkie ring, or snazzy shoes, or lush socks competed with this meta-message of financial modesty.

Jimmy could have gazed in the mirror each morning and asked: Do I look convincingly poor enough, today?

But he couldn't be utterly repulsive and still be admitted into homes.

He needed to appear appropriate to the task to get the appropriate result: sales and lots of them.

In this sense, for Jimmy there was a well demarcated front-stage and backstage, an on-stage and an off-stage. His front stage was penury and the backstage was wealth.

His on-stage was that beaten-up wagon, and the off-stage was that cool Cadillac.

Speaking of dramatic arcs, there are predictable crises that occur in the development of salespeople. At first, eager and clueless, they do exactly as they are told.

Before too long, they succeed because they follow instructions. They may soar to the top of the chart, ranking among the best sellers.

Then they fall into an inexplicable slump. Sales mysteriously elude them. They can't buy an order.

What's going on?

They get cocky and develop too much swagger. They get what one professional sales manager called, "sales breath." They signal that they're super-slick and super-savvy.

And soon enough, they start super-starving!

They have also probably changed their appearances.

I know a restaurant owner whose place is near the major studios in Burbank, California. Famously, he wears shorts to work, rain or shine, summer or winter.

Even by showbiz standards this attire is pretty daring, made more so by the fact this fellow isn't an Ambercrombie model. But he pays the bills and if he's losing any patrons because of those shorts, he might be gaining some out of respect for his dauntless desire to look beachy.

Back we go to the arc of sales achievement. Those sellers that start well and then slump, what's going on with them? Almost invariably, they've turned away from the basics. When their results hit rock bottom that's when they're open to constructive criticism.

And that invariably goes like this:

"You've become too smart for your own good. Go back to the basics and nothing more. Act like an eager rookie, following our script word for word. Then see that happens."

Typically, this will bring them back from the brink. Soon, they'll log new sales and they'll rise to the top once more.

Then, and you probably guessed it, the pattern will repeat. They'll become full of themselves, perhaps acting entitled, and a sales swoon will begin.

When it comes to clothing your clients may give you clues that you don't look the part, as my dad used to refer to dressing appropriately.

I had been doing public seminars at universities across the country and I adopted a simple uniform for myself. This saved me time and I could travel with fewer suitcases.

I wore a navy blue blazer and gray slacks, accompanied by a white or light blue oxford shirt and a striped necktie, typically in red and blue.

I think it looked sharp, and it was dressy enough but also casual enough at the same time. When I was invited to speak at companies, I wore the same thing.

Then my contact at a Seattle based financial company took me aside.

"We wear suits here, so you should too, if you want to fit in."

Immediately, upon returning home I went to Nordstrom and bought two conservative pinstriped, Italian tailored classics, one in dark blue and the other in dark gray.

The contract I had with that Seattle firm was the beginning of a consulting streak at multiple financial firms. And I developed a taste for traveling to London for three and four weeks at a time.

Their sales, across the city, started before Christmas, not after. So, I loaded-up on fantastic duds, including a number of double-breasted, Savile Row spectaculars.

All low key, mind you, but to the discerning eye they were clearly a cut way above the ordinary. Again, I bought them at a deep discount, up to 50% off.

This turned out to be what some call "investment dressing." Here's how.

The very best of the best suits I purchased was a silk navy blue. The fit was amazing. I was made for this ensemble.

I wore it, among four other great suits, each week at my client's site. By that time I had about twelve tremendous outfits, but I kept 5 at The Four Seasons Hotel in Houston, where I rented a suite by the month.

By the time I returned each Sunday night from my LA weekends, my suits would be cleaned and pressed and waiting for me in my bedroom closet, along with my shirts and ties and shoes.

When I drove into work, I looked tidy and like a million bucks.

This was very appropriate because I was consulting to a financial firm where looking sharp was the order of the day.

About 12 years after I finished that contract I was invited to consult at an international insurance firm headquartered in the Midwest.

I had been recommended by one of my manager-trainees at the Houston company. He positioned me as incredibly successful by describing that special blue suit.

"It was the most expensive, best looking suit I had ever seen!" he recalled.

With that testimonial, that suit helped me to snare a half-million dollar deal, a dozen years after I was last seen wearing it!

Of course, I got my wish, the one I revealed to you earlier.

I aspired to looking great, to signaling my success. I found a way of doing this and cleaning up. As I said it, above, "I didn't want to be pathetic. I wanted to be respected, dignified!"

And I didn't have to invest a second day in the vacuum cleaner business to accomplish it!

Clothing communicates!

We need to remember this as we go about our selling duties.

I know sellers who work only on the phone and by email, yet they insist on dressing-up for work, even if they're making calls from home!

"I know they can't see me unless I'm using video-conferencing," one seller says. "But I can see me! And dressing well makes me feel professional and I just can't get that buzz from staying in my pajamas."

He's wise enough to appreciate that we are an audience to ourselves, to our own appearances. So, when we're dressing for success, we're dressing in a way that reflects our professional and personal values.

We look good, we know it, and this makes us more confident, leading us to come across credibly, and persuasively.

But that frumpy guy was successful too. What about him?

Again, he dressed appropriately for his product, for his company, and for his intended audience.

His clothes made him feel-the-part that he was playing, and those clothes didn't compete with a productive definition of the situation.

He was smart enough to seem simple, and he got great satisfaction from playing this role five or six days a week.

His red and white carriage awaited him at the end of his toil, ready to convey his royal highness swiftly back to his castle, complete with golf course and other regal amenities.

His time among the commoners was well spent.

9

Meta:
Are You A Cherry Or A Pit?

Just because we can sell someone doesn't mean we should or we must.

These words might make you scratch your head.

After all, if you're in sales, the more the better, right? Whoever heard about a seller that thrived by NOT making sales?

You don't ring the cash register by turning people away. Yet I'm saying you should precisely do this, shunning various individuals and companies, because they aren't worth doing business with.

Each year I went through a ritual with my CPA. More or less at the last minute I'd see him for our annual tax time appointment. He would smile and shake his head as he saw me clutching jiffy bags filled with errant receipts and other documents.

I did my best to rubber band them into categories: restaurants, gasoline, parking, and the like. But I hadn't added them up.

I left that to him, which he was a whiz at, running a physical tape through his munching, crunching calculator.

Every year he'd insist there was a better path forward. I'd make an earlier appointment. I'd be more organized. I'd enter figures into a tax planner that would make his job faster and earlier.

The list went on and on. By no means was I an ideal client.

But I paid well, and he had been doing my taxes since he was a recent college grad and I was still in school, trying to minimize my taxes from my lucrative Time-Life sales and management job.

Adding up my pluses, even with my many minuses, I was still worth doing business with.

This is a calculus we need to perform BEFORE we put new clients on the books. Are they going to be a pleasure or a pain to work with? Most are a combination, as I was.

And if you're in business you have to take some bad with the good.

A passage from the *Tao Te Ching*, famous book of wisdom reflects this notion by asking:

What is a good man but a bad man's teacher? What is a bad man but a good man's work?

Seen this way, it is precisely that people are troubled, that they have problems that makes them need or want our solutions.

But we don't have to take all comers.

There will be about 20% or less of your customers that will give you 80% of your headaches.

How can you tell that you're dealing with one?

One type of problem person is the liar. For instance, if I had given bogus numbers to my CPA, figures that I did not or could not substantiate, then upon audit, he would have been professionally embarrassed or even sanctioned in an egregious case.

It's in his interest to separate the sleazes from stand-up people, clients he can count on to not bring his firm into disrepute.

This may seem too goody-two shoes, too idealistic, but as a professional he has responsibilities.

I delivered a major speech to a convention of executive recruiters. It was a hit, and the speech was videoed for later use by the franchisees in attendance.

Some of them inquired about bringing me in to consult at their individual locations. I agreed to perform a two-day needs assessment for a Connecticut based unit.

They fly me out and I interview managers about their practices, offering tips for improvement. Also, I determine whether there is more work to be done, the extent to which I need to return to do training and development.

The two-day inaugural visit stands is cost-justified. I deliver value by investing my time and by troubleshooting, as well as by spotting larger issues that should be addressed.

I receive value by being paid for my time and travel.

But there is a fairly solid presumption that if the initial engagement goes well, they'll retain me to return to implement the changes I've recommended, and that service will be contracted for, separately.

In this one case, I did my part. In the process I interviewed the two owners of the location and each spent some time bashing the other one's style.

It was a little unusual, but I took it in stride that one of my functions would be getting them on the same page.

At the end of my visit they confessed they were married, but they kept it from me and from others "for business purposes."

Suddenly, I felt I was being enlisted into palace intrigue for no constructive purpose. There was just something weird I felt about them after learning that they lied to me about this, of all things.

So, instead of coming back for an extended engagement, I told them upon my return to Los Angeles that we'd wrap our program up where we were.

We were done.

This is a perquisite of being in business for oneself. You can choose and un-choose your clients. What I want you to appreciate is when you are in sales you're also in business for yourself.

Typically, there will be a tomorrow. There is an expectation that you'll also service the account to an extent as well as to try to cross-sell and up-sell other profitable items.

A relationship isn't hit-and-run. What kind of relationship will it be?

We can't be certain, but I subscribe to the iceberg theory. That icy protrusion a captain sees sticking out of the water is dangerous. But what isn't seen is by orders of magnitude, worse.

The greatest mass of the danger lurks below the surface.

So the iceberg theory is stated this way: If what you can see is treacherous, what you cannot see is much worse.

If that couple lied about being married, what else would they lie about? And if I could take what they said at their word, how uncomfortable and dysfunctional would that be if we attempted to move forward?

I decided not to find out.

They were not pleased with my decision. I didn't call them liars. Vaguely, I said the project wasn't right for me, or something to that effect.

I was turning down some pretty serious money with that decision. But I comforted myself with this business truism:

Bad business pushes away good business.

If I forced myself to do an extended gig with them I would not be available to serve a better client if one came along.

As it happened, I signed another client soon after dismissing them. It was a branch of Transamerica, a prominent financial firm, that paid me more money, and I could service them locally, optimizing my time.

If I hadn't abbreviated the Connecticut connection, I would not have been as aggressive as I was in cultivating and closing Transamerica.

My contact there was from what I could see a person with integrity and we got along very well. Our relationship endured long past the end-date of our project and he became a positive reference for me, which earned me even more clients and more income.

Recently, I declined doing business with a firm whose principal owner was way too needy. He was slothfully slow in responding to my requests for information, but he insisted on getting from me instant replies to his messages and emails.

Well, you might say communication was a one-way street for him, a do as I say and not as I do proposition. It was inconvenient to say the least.

One client of mine, a very savvy fellow in Seattle, brought me in to his elite financial firm, where he was a Senior VP, to do some sales training.

Tony said to me as we were chatting at the airport one afternoon, "I've found life is too short to deal with unpleasant people."

He drew a bright, bold line. If you weren't civil and polite and dignified, you were out.

He wasn't dismissing me! He was sharing his philosophy, plainly and simply.

You might be thinking, as I admit I did, "Easy for you to say, your company is unique and rich! You can afford to rise above the crass and classless."

But if you endorse that notion I offered a minute ago, that bad business pushes out the good, then you'll probably appreciate that we really don't have time to feed problems.

We have to starve them, as management sage and my professor, Peter F. Drucker repeatedly said.

Who do we feed, then?

We need to feed opportunities.

The recruitment company was a problem. I starved it. Transamerica was an opportunity, and I fed it.

Once, I attended a training program for consultants. It was very useful, with some colorful and memorable takeaways.

The speaker said, when it comes to prospects and clients there are two kinds, cherries and pits. What most sellers do is waste their time with the pits and fail to invest enough time with the cherries.

That misallocation of time and effort is something he called, "pit polishing."

No matter how much effort we squander polishing pits to the highest sheen or gloss, the fact remains, now and forever, all we'll get are pits.

Maybe they were cherries once, but now they're pits and nothing will make them otherwise. What do we do with pits?

Toss them out, while seeking out, cultivating and harvesting genuine cherries.

So, the meta-question we need to be asking is:

Are you a cherry or a pit?

Was that recruiting firm a cherry or a pit? I'd say, it was mostly a pit in the iceberg is mostly a peril.

Whatever nutritious value they had to offer I sampled and then I moved on to snare an entire bag of cherries if you add together Transamerica and the other clients it led me to developing.

Yesterday, I was in touch with a financial firm that I was cultivating with an eye on creative a strategic alliance. We'd be partnering, so I wouldn't be working for them, or they for me.

We'd be working together toward the goal of creating and sharing profits.

Thomas Harris came up with a handy way of describing relationships that applies to this and to other situations. He called it Transactional Analysis.

He said there are three basic complementary relationships: (1) Parent to Parent, (2) Adult to Adult, and (3) Child to Child.

It's easy to converse and to get along when we are talking to each other on the same level. You know this if you've ever attended a school fundraiser or sporting event and you're chatting with other parents. You have the same issues, and when you are all wearing your "parent hats" you're breezing through the occasion, quite nicely and effortlessly.

But if one of you pulls rank and dons an Expert hat, posing as a super-parent, a know-it-all, conflicts ensue.

I know, having written the book, *101 Things Parents Should Know Before Volunteering to Coach Their Kids' Sports Teams.*

If you felt the slightest twinge of discomfort reading the last line, then you know how it feels to experience being talked-down to.

Well, yesterday when I was conferring with my would-be partner, he simply wouldn't allow us to stay on an Adult-to-Adult level. Insisting on being a superior party to our transaction, he kept asking me to supply unnecessary details instead of agreeing, in principle, to the big picture we should be aiming at.

He was having a Parent to Child conversation when we really needed and could only make progress with a, Adult to Adult one.

He didn't have the communication sensitivity required to sense that was a problem and if it persisted, we weren't going to make progress, now or in the future.

I saw the issue and concluded he was simply too stupid to educate, to be a person with whom to meta-communicate.

So, I wished him a good day and moved on to another prospect.

I suppose I could have interrupted him with a smile in my voice while asking:

Are you always going to be a problem like this?

He would have asked, "Like what?"

Well, it seems we're missing the big picture while focusing on minor details. Let me ask you this: Assuming I can provide you with all the details you need, do you see us moving forward?

This is a fish-or-cut bait-disqualifying question. Or you could call it a crystal ball question. It borders on rudeness because it is so direct and to the point.

But we are really asking are you a cherry or a pit?

If we have laid a foundation with someone, I believe it is a fair question. Is there a there-there, or a here-here?

Is it my imagination or are we stuck at square one?

I want to offer you another rule of thumb when it comes to detecting pits that you may mistake for cherries.

There is an old world expression for predicting failure in a marriage between individuals:

A tumultuous courtship signals a more tumultuous marriage to come.

Meaning, if they're arguing like this now, just wait for the vows: It will only get worse!

Sure, there are exceptions, as in Shakespeare's "Taming of The Shrew" and its popular Broadway incarnation, "Kiss Me Kate." They nearly killed each other but seemed to finally succumb to marital bliss.

It makes a great show, but it's not often replicated in real life, especially in commercial contexts.

Recently, I partnered with an organization to host my seminar. Their role was to promote by email to their extensive membership, to process registrations, and to split the proceeds with me.

I devised the customized program, and wrote all of the texts promoting it, including the email invitation, and arranged the meeting venue particulars. I also volunteered to make a few highly targeted calls to the best leads I could detect from their list.

From beginning to this very moment—this case is actually happening now—they have dragged their feet. It took them eight months to agree to participate and they have been extremely late in sending out our mailers.

So much so, it looks like we'll have to postpone or cancel the engagement, entirely.

We may have missed the mark in other ways, partly my fault, but there has been such a dearth of cooperation and the timely feedback it could have given me, that we have been incapable of making mid-course adjustments and corrections.'

They're been a congenial and incompetent partner. And I suspected they would be unreliable from the beginning.

(Still, I ventured ahead, which we'll get to in a second . . .)

What tipped me off? What should have nailed it for me that they would be far less than ideal, and actually a waste of my time and effort?

They were initially very enthusiastic about the partnering concept. But they procrastinated. When I pushed for mini-commitments, they retreated. Excuses piled up. Vacations came around and the board of directors needed to be consulted. Weeks and months passed.

Again, what was the clue?

There was an inverse correlation between the enthusiasm and the progress. I was hearing all happy talk, but seeing no action.

They were too agreeable, yet never really committing time and resources.

They are Smile Suckers. They smile and we're the suckers that mistake congeniality for genuine interest.

You see this in Hollywood and showbiz. Nobody wants to offend anyone, because: "Never kick a pup, because that pup grows up."

You could be a nobody today and tomorrow make a

hit movie or You Tube video by financing it on a credit card and shooting it on your iPhone.

So, everyone is nicey-nicey, best of pals, but they're killing you with kindness, with compliments, with verbal bouquets.

Meantime, you're not getting anywhere, time passes, and deals don't get done.

The test of a business relationship is performance, not platitudes.

I said I'd address the fact that I saw these signals of non-performance early on. Yet I decided to stay the course, to float through the doldrums, and to accept the promises of performance at face value.

And I had some good reasons to hang in there with them. I saw them as a prototype of the sort of partner I wanted in the future. Their organization could easily be cloned, there are branches everywhere, and we we're innovating in content and using a special technology platform for content delivery.

In a phrase, there is a big upside.

But people need to play their proper roles. Just as it's impossible to have both sides of a conversation, each party has to hold up her end of it.

We can only sell when people buy! If they balk or refuse to cooperate or make transactions too financially or emotionally expensive, we need to retreat.

Will this partner of mine become a juicy, plump, life sustaining cheery, a late bloomer?

Or was it simply a pit, pretending to be a cherry.

Very soon, I'll find out!

10

Finding Your Meta-Sales Voice

Two of the best salespeople I have known had the worst voices. One worked for me at Time-Life Books, and another worked with me at a CPA firm.

How would I describe them? They were raspy and generally unpleasant to hear. But they sold, nonetheless.

In each setting there were also people on the sales team with "announcers voices." You know the type. They're resonant, and actually a pleasure to hear.

They failed. Go figure.

My point is there has to be a match between who you are, how you sound, what you say, what you're selling, and the audience to whom you are selling.

Plus, there's the Meta-Factor.

Ben, at Time-Life was an adept art bookseller. He loved these fine books and his voice, gravelly as it was didn't get in the way of his florid, enticing descriptions.

In fact, he sounded 100% sincere, partly because he

wasn't smooth enough to sound like your typical seller. You could say his was a Meta-Voice!

It said, "I'm not your typical seller, so don't reject me as you would, them."

His Meta-factor, that un-salesy voice, was his signature strength that rose above the sales medium, enabling him to start and then to finish at great length, his sales chats.

There is behavioral research that provides a useful insight into this phenomenon of being less than perfect and having an audience reward you for it. It is called "The Pratfall Effect."

We don't like perfect people, and when it comes to selling, we outright distrust them. You've heard of the warning to beware of "Silver-Tongued Devils," those that are a little too polished and too articulate in their sales delivery.

The Pratfall Effect says if you make a glaring error, or even say, "I'm not very good at this—pardon me," you'll score points with listeners. They'll identify with you.

A member of a very famous political family got up from his chair to deliver a speech and his meal promptly fell into his lap.

He made a self-effacing joke about it, saying he was really a clod, and the audience laughed with him and loved him for his humility. They expected to be in the presence of an utter stiff!

This is so powerful, this Pratfall effect, that sellers build it into their spiels. In-home sellers learn to request a glass of water from their hosts. This is to induce cooperation but it also says "I need a little help with this, if you don't mind."

Not only do prospects not mind, they like becoming "part of the act."

So, find your Meta-Selling Voice. If you're smooth, introduce a croak here and there.

And if you're a little rough and raspy, don't change a thing!

Imperfect is Perfect.

11

Meta:
How Much Money Will You Make?

Over the course of 20+ years I've delivered hundreds of sales and sales management seminars.

Do you know what the touchiest subject has been? Here are some hints.

It hasn't been about gender. Do men or women sell more effectively to their own or to other sexes? Though you have to admit, this is an interesting and provocative variable.

It hasn't been about race. Do people prefer to buy based on someone's racial or ethnic appearance? Also fascinating, this is especially volatile in the times in which we live.

The sexiest, most sizzling and most taboo topic has been compensation. That's right: money and exactly how sellers earn it.

If there has been one area of discussion where the spirits whisper to me, "tread lightly," this is it. It is a meta-topic that informs almost all selling and staffing behaviors.

We know there are certain broad behavioral tendencies based on whether we are paid on a straight salary or a straight commission basis. As stereotypes would have it, salaried sellers are lazy. And commissioned sellers are high-energy hustlers that will say and do anything to close deals.

I'm being facetious here. Yet there are lots of sales managers and business owners that use these caricatures and others.

What you need to discover is under what sort of compensation plan you work most effectively. Negotiating the right fit can mean the difference between feasting and starving, being utterly stressed out or being in a relative state of bliss.

Here's what we know. We get what we measure, and we get what we reward.

At Time-Life Books our sales comp plan evolved over time. At first, it offered a base hourly wage. On top of that was a commission paid for each "sale" that went out the door.

Our sales were agreements to review the lead books in our libraries on a 10-day trial. So, no money changed hands, at least right away.

When recipients got the books and liked them they sent in their money. If they didn't like them, they sent them back by return mail.

Sellers needed to create enough interest to get the books out the door, but if they were paid for later or returned, it didn't affect their paychecks. They were paid for the books that went out, not the ones that were paid for or were returned.

We could have side-by side-sellers, each sending out fifty books a week. They'd receive exactly the same pay, even if one rep's sales "stuck" and were almost all paid for, and the other one's were returned en masse.

The first seller would be far and away more valuable to the company than the second. Yet as long as we simply measured books shipped, we risked encouraging both reps, equally.

In its wisdom, the company revised the pay plan. Still, the same base hourly wage was paid. Also, commissions were paid for books shipped, albeit at a lower amount.

But a third feature was added. Reps received variable "trailing" commissions six weeks later from the books that stuck.

It was at this stage where the good sellers and the bad became visible to all concerned. Because the trailing commissions were tiered, this meant the higher the percentage of books that were paid for the higher ones commissions were, per sold book.

Again, reps #1 and #2 could have identical paychecks at the end of each week as books were shipped. But six weeks later, one could be swimming in cash, while the other looked on in agony.

At first, sellers resisted the new plan, saying: "I can't control who pays and who doesn't!" But this was wrong.

On that initial sales call, by emphasizing: "you're going to want to keep it and collect the rest of the library," our retention numbers went up, as a group.

We had far more impact on profitability than we at first realized.

It didn't take much to make those collections soar. Just by adding a line or two to the "confirmation" portion of our initial sales call, we could have a huge impact on outcomes.

Especially helpful was inserting this tie-down question as a finale: "And if you like the book you will keep it, right?"

If prospects wavered or sounded less than convincing, we buttressed sale by offering more good reasons to buy it. If that wasn't effective, we canceled our own order before writing it up.

"Well, why don't we just put this on hold and check back with you another time," we'd say.

Those that had no genuine buying intention sounded relieved. We saved time and effort and expense in mailing a book that could be lost or returned.

I offer this extended example of a comp plan because it stands for the idea that sellers will do what is rewarded, period. So, companies have to be very careful to incentivize the results they want, while reducing the habit of reinforcing the wrong behaviors.

Let's shift contexts for a moment to dramatize how management can engineer exactly the wrong results. For some time, customer service reps were rewarded based on the length of their customer calls.

If the "average call length" were brief and met standards, reps would receive bonuses, raises, and promotions. If calls dragged on and on, reps were punished, or at least barred from receiving additional rewards.

What companies did not do is teach reps how to agreeably and pleasantly manage call length. They were left to using their own devices, some of which were very crude.

In addition to saying, "Got to go," and "We need to wrap this up!" some reps would force customers to call back to ask their additional questions.

This forced other reps to carry the load, while it frustrated and perplexed customers who expected one-call satisfaction.

Instead of reducing customer dissatisfaction this renegade practice increased it.

I devised very supportive and totally invisible ways to make calls, on average, 25% shorter, but better. This alleviated the problem.

But the fact remains, when it comes to compensation, we get what we measure. And often, it's all we get.

I mentioned above that the stereotype of the commission-only seller is someone that will say and do anything to get a commission. On one level, being exclusively focused on results isn't a bad thing.

Of course, we don't want to misrepresent or to offend, so sellers need to self-censor. Managers that believe they can control through micro-management how exactly commission sellers sell, are deluding themselves.

If they want that sort of control, then they need to pay a salary. A salary signifies that there are certain procedures and busy-work that must be tended to in order for salespeople to earn their pay.

Failing to pay a salary makes sellers feel more like independent contractors than employees. And the operative word in that first term is, "independent."

What do you need to perform at your best? What sort of pay plan suits you?

Answer this accurately, and you'll do yourself a big favor, as well as everyone around you, including your employer.

The answer can change over the course of your employment at a company and definitely over the course of a career.

Students that sell part-time may be misfits for a straight commission plan. They have to pay vital bills and have only a few hours to dedicate each day or week to the task.

We can't in good conscience ask them to "bet the farm" each time they show up for work. Not selling isn't a risk they can afford to take. They could be betting the rent or their meals on whether they succeed.

Speaking of "weather," as I write these words a hurricane is making its way up the East Coast of the U.S. Businesses are being shuttered, and some homes evacuated.

People on a straight commission income plan are going to be pummeled by the economic fallout of this storm. When they work, they earn. When nature strikes, they're defenseless.

That hypothetical student will be without funds for a reason completely out of his or her hands. Quite possibly, if they were on a salary, their employer would still pay them during the bad weather, or offer an advance against future income.

But an independent contractor type will be up a river or in a storm surge without a paddle.

Straight commission can be a peachy plan for people in the right circumstances. In my speeches and seminars I refer to a salesman I met at my client's Houston site.

He was on a straight commission plan, selling bond funds to institutional investors, such as banks and college endowments.

He went for a full 10 months without getting his first sale!

Can you imagine what that feels like, earning zero income while you're desperately trying to score? What do you tell your friends and intimates when they ask how the job is going?

I infer he had some outside support or his own nest egg he could use to survive. Even if he figured the money part out, the emotional costs he suffered had to be huge.

Unless you're a Zen monk, eating "nothingburgers" for 10-months is an unrelenting blow to one's self-esteem.

Finally, he broke through. Sumitomo Bank, head-quartered in Japan, awarded this downtrodden soul with his first order.

Guess what his commission was?

One million dollars!

It was a large deal, as you can imagine. And the amount he earned was a percentage of the dollar amount that his company charged.

I use this story in a number of ways. It shows that a straight commission pay plan can be a wonderful thing and very, very rewarding.

But a number of other factors need to be in place. First, you need to work for a company that will hold up its end of the bargain and actually pay you what you earn when those sporadic, but huge deals come through.

There are firms that will "cap" your commissions at a certain amount. This is one of the greatest oddities in the annals of sales compensation.

In theory, your employer wants you to earn as much as you possibly can. Reason: When you succeed, your employer succeeds, as well.

So, why would an employer say we want you to excel, but if you do, we'll stop you from earning even more at that point?

Yet there are firms that say and do exactly that.

Billionaire Ross Perot worked for IBM and was its best seller. He was so good that one year he earned his annual sales quota at the end of January.

He capped out, and could not earn another penny above that cap based on company policy. He thought this was absurd.

Challenging IBM to alter its plan, Big Blue refused.

And so, Perot quit and started his own hugely successful enterprise, becoming a billionaire in the process.

Needless to say IBM lost its very best sales worker.

Worse, they lost a living, breathing, highly achieving role model that was walking the walk, demonstrating it can be done!

Records can be broken and made anew.

How much is it worth to have an active super-seller on your team?

See, this is the first question anyone must ask when taking a commission-only job. Can it be done? Is it being done, now?

Perot was proof.

That million dollar earning financial salesman worked in a bullpen next to other sellers that were scoring. Not as much, but they were earning. So, he had his proof.

If you're on a straight commission plan does this mean the company will not invest in your success? Are you totally on your own, in a bad way?

Saying this a different way, when an employer is out of pocket to you, having paid you some sort of guaranteed wage, then they have money on the line. They don't want to lose it.

Thus they'll be inclined to provide you with enough quality leads to earn back what they have forked out.

If they haven't invested, they're inclined to fudge on giving what you need to survive and to thrive.

There are exceptions, and I believe that financial client of mine was one of them. They needed to support the sales team, and they did in various ways other than by providing a guaranteed income.

But my experience tells me it is useful to make them pay something, even a nominal amount, up front. The more they're committed to paying the more they're committed to retrieving it.

And that works in a seller's favor.

Recall the Time-Life example. They went from paying large up-front dollars to paying even larger back-end dollars in the form of trailing commissions. Still, they offered a set salary and a nominal up-front spiff for successful efforts to secure 10-day trials.

Their plan, and this is why I use it as a touchstone, had something for every type of seller and circumstance.

The struggling student received something guaranteed to pay room and board. The risk-taker, or professional seller knew if she or he did a good job on the back end, significant money would be earned at that point.

Guaranteed pay, plus the potential for earning significant commissions that are not capped, seems to be an almost ideal plan.

There are lots of versions. Where employers are totally committed to a commission-only plan, I encourage them to offer a keep-all-over variant.

I sold ballpoint pens while in graduate school. They were stamped 49 cents on the barrel. I "bought" them from my employer at 16 cents apiece. What I chose to sell them for was completely up to me.

I set my own profit margins. I could have sold them for 17 cents or for 48 cents or for anything in between.

The price point I chose was 33 cents. So, for each 16-cent pen I bought, I earned 17 cents when I sold it.

I made more money on each deal than my employer did!

Now, that was a great pay plan. I cleaned up, bought a new car, and was one flush grad student. I also taught classes at school and earned that way, so I was quite well off.

What I liked about the pen plan was that I was in charge. I loved getting big margins. That was a thrill in itself and a tribute to my sales savvy.

I could come and go as I pleased, based on my other commitments.

So, you need to look at each plan and ask yourself what do I really need? I had my teacher's pay, so I didn't need the assurance of a set salary. I felt like a gambler that was playing with the casino's money.

That job worked out because I didn't feel any major pressures to perform, other than internal ones. The wolf wasn't at the door.

Had he been, I would have sought a salaried plan.

The temple in which the Oracle of Delphi dwelled bore an inscription: Know thyself.

I say this applies to knowing what type of pay plan turns you on or off as a salesperson.

It is a crucial meta-consideration that can nudge you on to success or make you spin your wheels.

Choose wisely!

12

But The SX-70 Is A Great Camera, Isn't It?

Let me provide a case in point from my client archives that shows the power of Meta Selling.

Polaroid was one of the first American high-tech companies. Its instant photography cameras enabled consumers to see their photos in about a minute as they developed in the palm of their hands. Until that time, people had to cart their film to places that would send them out for processing and printing. Typically, that took several days to accomplish.

Toward the beginning of the digital age, I was a consultant to Polaroid's customer service centers in Cambridge, Massachusetts and around the country. At quite a sizable cost, hundreds of people fielded thousands of calls each day, mostly about poorly developing film and cameras that were malfunctioning.

I was called in to see if Polaroid could transform what was a cost center into a profit center. The bold question they asked me was this:

"Can we sell something new to customers that are phoning us to complain?"

What a great question, especially if you're a communication theorist with a Ph.D. and with years of sales and service consulting experience under your belt.

I said I'd be happy to study the idea and make some recommendations.

I determined it was possible, if done very delicately and with great conversational precision. It would take a special protocol for handling the call, including a new bridging device to transition from problem solving to selling.

I scripted this conversation while selecting three auxiliary products that could be sold at a profit to nearly every caller. What was left was designing a training program to get customer service representatives to implement the techniques I developed.

We took a pilot group and I taught them what to say, exactly when to say it, and even the tones with which to say it. I came to call these components, The Three T's: Text, Tone & Timing.

Our results were amazing. About 50% of the people that were offered an auxiliary product bought one. This happened during the same call in which they announced their complaint.

Naturally, I had some trepidation about selling to angry people. If I didn't plan this properly, and if calls weren't handled well, it would be like adding gasoline to a fire and then fanning the flames.

Imagine what an aware, irate customer could say: "Here I am really teed off because my camera won't work, and you want to sell me something to go with it before you've even fixed it?"

Poorly executed, this campaign could become a public relations disaster.

"Polaroid's stuff breaks: Want fries with that?"

"It's one thing to sell extra stuff to satisfied customers. But trying to sell unsatisfied ones? That's absolutely tone deaf."

As you can imagine, a lot was at stake, so I had to really put on my thinking cap to finesse this challenge.

I conceived the conversation as having two major parts: (1) Part one handled the complaint part of the call. Here, CSRs explain how and where to send the camera for repair. (2) Part two would sell them something new, one of 35 possible auxiliary products Polaroid stocked.

The real trick was transitioning smoothly from (1) to (2).

We could not get away with an abrupt change such as this:

"So, if you'll simply send that to the address I gave you then we'll get it back to you within 7-10 working days. Would you be interested in a leather carrying case for your SX-70? We have them at only $39.95."

I have to be kidding, right? That would never work. People might say, if they were kind, "Please fix my camera first, and then we'll see."

I decided to do a little analysis of the people that were calling in for help. What were their emotions?

They were upset. But that word wasn't precise enough. They were disappointed. The camera or the film let them down. They had high hopes for a trouble free experience.

They may have blamed themselves for choosing this pricey piece of technology.

I determined I needed to draft a message that reminded them of the wisdom of their original purchase. This would be the transition smoothing the way from sour to satisfaction.

They needed to be in an upbeat mood to buy again, especially on the spot. How could I change their mood in an instant?

Here's what I came up with:

"So, if you'll simply send that to the address I gave you then we'll get it back to you within 7-10 working days. But the SX-70 is a great camera, isn't it?"

What happened next was utterly magical.

It is a great camera. We've had so much fun with it. We took it to Disney World last year and got some great shots with it . . ."

Almost to a person, callers endorsed the idea that the SX-70 is a great camera. Once they opened-up and started singing its praises, all CSRs had to do was listen, agree, and occasionally chime-in.

Then, they were trained to say:

Most people don't know that we've designed a nice leather carrying case for it that has an over the shoulder strap. It only runs $39.95, and I'll be happy to send one out to you, if you like."

We had similar texts for the flash attachment and for the photo album with specially sized indentations for Polaroid pictures.

CSRs could choose the item they thought would be most fitting for the customer they were speaking to.

This case represents and astonishingly effective use of Meta Selling. By inserting the prompt, But the SX-70 is a great camera, isn't it?" Reps were able to instantly change the mood of the customer from one of disappointment to one of great appreciation.

That statement induced customers to re-sell themselves on Polaroid's quality. This was a necessary precursor to getting them to buy an added item, on the spot.

The phrase acted to open a parallel conversation with customers. Suddenly, they were recalling and therefore reliving joyous moments, brought to them by Polaroid.

Not only did the customer's voice go from "down in the dumps" to one of elation, CSR voices, soared, as well. Imagine fielding hundreds of negative calls every day. That's hard to handle without being bitten by the negative bug, oneself.

But suddenly, they could make customers sing! And when they sang the praises of Polaroid, reps could bask in it because they were part of that special company, with its special products.

So, a happy communication loop was created with the line, "But the SX-70 is a great camera, isn't it?"

Miraculously, no customer expressed negativity about being offered the extra product. And interestingly, those that bought became even more committed to the wisdom of their original purchase and to Polaroid.

Surprisingly, the people that complained weren't the customers. They were the customer service reps that were asked to put these new techniques to work.

Some felt the techniques were "manipulative," that I had tapped a dark art in developing them!

Recall, these were CSRs, not salespeople, so some felt they didn't sign-on to be persuaders. Today, this concern sounds quaint, given how many hats people are expected to wear in the workplace.

In many cases, these folks had been awarded "tenure" by Polaroid, which is a story, in itself.

Edwin Land founded Polaroid. He was a brilliant scientist and Harvard dropout who would generate hundreds of patents and personally inspire and mentor recent tech luminaries such as Apple's Steve Jobs. He would later receive an honorary doctorate from Harvard, and dub himself Dr. Land, which most media were happy to use as a title.

Land invented instant photography and located his company on the Charles River, just a few blocks from the MIT campus, and a couple of miles downstream from Harvard. He recruited and placed into responsible positions the smartest people he could find, including many female graduates from Smith College.

He modeled Polaroid after a university, calling its buildings a "campus," one of the first companies to do that. He also decided that the best way to reward workers wasn't with money. It was better to provide them life-time employment, also known as tenure, so they'd never have to worry about losing their jobs.

Free from the pressures of corporate politics and the threat of personal privation, Polaroid "associates" could actually turn down, with impunity, assignments they didn't want to perform.

With the mandate management gave me, I built an unbelievably profitable program that fulfilled its mission of transforming the customer service costs centers into profit centers. This was a major career achievement for me, and a genuine advancement in customer service and selling "science."

But the people in those centers were empowered to undo the program by refusing to follow it.

They may have worked in corporations, with corporations, and through corporations, but not for corporations.

They were autonomous.

I was chagrinned at the idea that I could use extraordinary inventiveness to create a process innovation, indeed a breakthrough in both service and selling with huge profit implications, yet have it be shunted aside by the rank and file.

With their knowledge workers, Polaroid, an innovation company, had succeeded in creating a cadre of workers that could stymie innovation. And when doing so, they couldn't be reprimanded or be terminated.

As part of the planned program, I met with senior management and reported on the progress of the program. I asked if it was true that they would not "make them use" the new techniques that the firm bought and paid for. I wanted to hear it from the horse's mouth.

And that's what they said. The honchos also mentioned that they wanted me to come back on a monthly basis over the course of a year to try to gently persuade these tenured knowledge workers to use the methods I had developed.

Busy with a slate of other high profile companies such as Xerox, which had its own vaunted sales force and sales training program, I declined.

Polaroid was an extreme case of what I encountered at a number of firms until about 2005, as I said. Employees felt and acted as if they could pick and choose work methods they liked, turning up their noses at others, as if they were in a cafeteria line.

Fearful of wrongful termination lawsuits, corporations hewed to the most extreme mavericks that could infect and distract work teams, seemingly with impunity.

Polaroid, unknown to me at the time I was brought in, had recently forced Dr. Land into retirement. Because tenure was his baby, and many people bristled over his departure, managers were very cautious about generating resistance from the employees he left behind.

But this notion that knowledge workers are authorities unto themselves was widespread.

At a software company where I consulted, there was a technical support worker who would begin to help people that called in about flaws in their products. He would veer off-script into lengthy religious sermons, insisting callers take to heart his spiritual exhortations.

That firm was paralyzed with fear that he would accuse it of being anti-Divine, so they reluctantly turned a deaf ear to his missives.

What happened to Polaroid?

I asked myself, how could a publicly funded company permit its people to choose less profitable work methods when it had paid for research and development of better methods that had proven to be effective and hugely profitable?

Consistent with my predictions, it went from being highly profitable to eventual bankruptcy.

Part of its demise is attributable to the fact that it couldn't quickly adapt to changing market conditions or to the demands of digital photography.

I must believe knowledge workers who were empowered to choose their own dysfunctional methods, while declining improved designs, were also to blame for the decline of that former icon of innovation.

I share this case with you to show how Meta Selling can have phenomenal impacts. But also, some of this wizardry can be so advanced, so state of the art in communication theory, that it can feel threatening, simply because it seems capable of achieving the impossible.

13

Controlling Your Self-Talk When You Fail

Yesterday, while my wife and kids were at a movie they had eagerly waited to see, I was having a chat with a retailer of customized furniture.

In addition to selling his own creations in a touristy beach area, he also features art and various objects fashioned by locals that he sells on consignment.

Happily, he had decided to display about 12 of my wife's original oil paintings. I have to say, upon bringing them into his store, I could appreciate them all the more. They're colorful, ranging from abstract-modern to impressionistic.

Some feature sailboats, one of her favorite images. Others are non-representational, and all of them looked great in that environment.

This had all come together quite by accident. I stopped by his store when I was returning books to the nearby library. His space had been empty for a few months, and suddenly it was occupied so I peeked in.

We talked furnishings and other things and it really didn't occur to me that her paintings would be a good fit, until I had left. I popped in the next day and mentioned her art, gave him her web site, and by the following day, the paintings were ready to install.

I wasn't selling him as much as partnering with him to display her art. Really, I'm just a go-between, a contact for him and a deliveryman for her.

Yet I left feeling on top of the world because in its way this alliance is a genuine breakthrough. She has had showings in various places, but having a retail platform that could lead to cultivating an art clientele hasn't happened, until now.

I love selling and I've closed some very large deals resulting in significant income to me. Yet this is just as exciting in its way.

Naturally, my first thought after being elated was that I should multiply this success.

I can find other spots for her to show her work. This happy self-talk and the vision of having many alliances of this sort was making me euphoric.

And this is one of the joys of selling. It's great fun when we succeed, and success builds on itself. We're eager to do again that which just electrified us and delivered value to others.

Unfortunately, when we fail we're likely to start a downward spiral of defeat that can sap our souls and make trying to succeed seem fruitless and punishing. In this regard, selling is truly a manic-depressive occupation.

"The best of times and the worst of times" happen as a cycle, repeatedly.

We need to become aware of our self-talk, especially when we're not getting the results we want. And crucially, we have to stop that inner dialogue when it feeds on itself.

The good news is we can do it.

I live on a boat channel. You might envision it as an extended back yard. We use it as a gigantic saltwater swimming pool.

We distend a ladder from our dock and enter a wild natural environment. It's unpredictable. An octopus lives on the quiet side of the dock, and I've seen videos of the creatures that swim around the channel, itself.

It's not quite the Discovery Channel or Wild Kingdom, but it certainly isn't your typical suburban swimming pool, either. We've seen seals, and of course, passing boats which are the biggest hazard, though occasional.

For about six months of the year, we can brave the temperature fairly easily. Considering the ocean's record warming trend, this has become easier over the last few years.

But around the middle of September, it doesn't get icy, but it can feel like it.

Whatever my mood is before I enter the water, I know one thing. It will change in a split second when my body merges with it. Instantly, I'm in the NOW.

I swim to the other side of the channel at almost full-speed. If it's cold, I never really get used to it.

About 15 or 20 minutes later, having done about three roundtrips, I climb out and take a cool shower. At that point, I'm feeling quite alive, and genuinely refreshed.

Often I'll combine a jog of a mile with swimming. Together, the two make me feel transcendental, other-worldly.

My point is I have learned that this exercise routine, especially coldwater swimming, stops my inner dialogue. If I have been ruminating over a missed sale or a deal that suddenly went sour, my feelings will have changed by the time I climb that aluminum ladder and leave Sea World.

If I'm thinking anything by the time I shiver to the shower, it's, "I feel great!" or "That was fantastic!"

The experience predictably and reliably resets my emotions.

If you're in sales, you need this, or its equivalent.

It is a momentum changer. When things are going great and you're selling well, leave it alone. Don't analyze it. Don't discuss it.

Like a pitcher that is hurling a no-hitter, it's best to just keep doing what you're doing. No need to stop, to do a victory dance or anything else. Simply continue.

All too soon that being-in-the-zone, I-can-do-no-wrong feeling will pass, by itself. Don't push it.

When you lose, you experience a setback, your mood is dark and your prospects are dim, that's when you need a reset of the type I've described. Mine is physical and it has obvious health benefits.

The key to slump busting is to change your routine. That immersion in cold water does it for me. I suppose you could take a cold shower and get the same shock value.

But if you read my situation, there is genuine survival on the line. Who knows what critter might want to take a bite out of me or strangle me with its tentacles?

Isn't this fun?

You can accomplish the same by joining a martial arts dojo. Sparring against highly skilled opponents will also put you smack into the middle of NOW.

I suppose on an unconscious level, the sales blues pale next to real survival threats. Who cares that you missed scoring with that prospect.

That's a lot better than missing a block when a fist is flying at your face!

Vigorous exercise summons deep survival programs.

Also, if we're going to beat ourselves up, better to do it constructively through physical exertion than psychologically, through self-downing.

Want to do penance for that missed sale where you forgot to close or failed to mention the most important benefit?

Do fifty pushups, now!

Take a lap!

This is how my sports coaches "punished" us. They did it with more conditioning! And that conditioning made us tougher.

How do you know you need an exercise break? There are several potential triggers.

Ironically, when your body feels a little achy-breaky, that's a peachy opportunity to put things in motion. You'd think exercising is what you should avoid when all is not perfect, right?

Wrong, You'll probably feel better afterwards because you'll forget about your aches and pains and you'll feel a surge of endorphins with a surge of pride that you didn't feel like doing it.

But you did it, anyway!

I keep free weights below my desk a few inches from my feet. They're always beckoning. And without notice, when I have a few seconds or feel poorly or just cranky, I'll do a few repetitions.

Right now, I'm going to do some curls.

I'm back! Two minutes have transpired and my posture is better. I breathed deeply.

I'm awake, I'm alive, and I feel fantastic!

Someone I worked with a while back suggested that affirmation I just uttered. Once more:

I'm awake, I'm alive, and I feel fantastic!

Go ahead. Say it now. It's your turn.

This is the sort of positive self-talk you need to use when you're succumbing to the Dark Side.

Guess what I'm feeling as I complete my icy swims? That's right, I'm awake, I'm alive, and I feel fantastic.

Will simply saying this have the same effect as taking those bracing dips? If you don't have an ocean merely a few steps away, it's worth a try.

Thoughts are routines, they have a momentum all their own. Have you ever awoken in the middle of the night, racked with worry? Maybe you have unpaid bills, or you're concerned about an upcoming presentation.

One bad thought leads to the next. Before long, you're "awfulizing," as psychologist Albert Ellis calls it.

"It's just awful that this bozo jerked me around for two months and then he bought from someone else," you could be telling yourself. Ellis teaches people to question these dramatic conclusions.

What makes it awful? You make it awful. Sure, it isn't fun. Your task should be changing "awful" to "mildly uncomfortable."

Tell yourself, "It's mildly uncomfortable when clients waste my time and then don't buy. But it comes along with being in sales."

Changing your extreme emotions for milder ones is a key to getting over what's bothering you, and doing so, quickly.

You've probably heard of affirmations. These are key phrases that you can repeat to feel better and on top of your game.

Here's one I like:

I am worthy of all good things.

Here's another:

I'm really good at this.

I particularly like the second one because it is exactly the opposite of what we feel when we fail to make a sale. Then we feel inept, out of our depth, incapable of succeeding.

At that point we need to remind ourselves of how well fitted to the task we really are. Of course, quickly earning the next agreement will probably accomplish this.

Affirmations are bridges to that next deal. They shorten the journey and put us in the proper mood to recover.

Let's say you're on a hot streak. One person after the next is buying from you. This is like seeing the next prospect with a telescope. It looks so close you can touch it.

But only one significant failure can turn that telescope the other way around. Suddenly, the next deal is way over the horizon, a tiny speck if you can detect it at all.

We're speaking of perceptions now. These are emotional assessments we make when we're winning or losing. The feelings can take on a life of their own, attracting more business to us like a magnet, or repelling it, making it go farther away, out of reach.

You've heard the expressions that support this phenomenon:

Nothing succeeds like success.

If you think you can, you're right. And if you think you can't, you're right.

When you're hot you're hot, and when you're not, you're not.

All of these point to momentum, which is one of the laws of nature. A body in motion stays in motion, and a body at rest remains at rest.

Specifically, we can't succumb to what sales guru Zig Ziglar called, "stinkin' thinkin'," which is also the title of one of my books.

When we're not succeeding we tend to unconsciously tell ourselves three things, according to psychologist Martin Seligman:

(1) Bad things are personal. (2) Bad things are pervasive. (3) Bad things are permanent.

"I didn't get that sale because I'm a lousy salesperson." That's personalizing the defeat, making it about us as human beings. Often we have very little if anything to do with a sales rejection, and thus have no good reason to take it, personally.

"Nobody is buying out there." I've weathered at least 3 if not 4 economic recessions and each time it's tempting to conclude that all commerce has stopped. We may be experiencing a slowdown or less activity, but some people are still doing things.

"This business is doomed. It will never be what it once was." Things change. Technologies come and go and we need to continually learn and adjust. So, to say it won't be what it once was, is almost a given.

But it could be better in other ways. Economist Schumpeter coined a term that you may have heard in use over the last few years: "creative destruction."

The new tends to "destroy" the old in certain ways, wringing out inefficiencies while bringing in efficiencies. In developing countries the advent of the washing machine utterly changed people's lives, usually for the better.

Suddenly, they saved loads of time. They were free to work at other things that required attention and to enjoy more leisure.

But it did alter the social lives of people that would gather by the waterway to do their washing and to chat. In that sense, the new technology killed off something cultural that was highly valued.

All businesses are doomed if we take the longest view. They will cease to serve the needs that they were first organized to serve. As with buggy whips, the disappearance of horse driven carriages made the former obsolete.

As a seller, you can't be a Pollyanna and assume your company and its products and services will always be a good fit for buyers. Yesterday's features and benefits may be unwanted by today's buyers.

Instead of awfulizing about this we need to adjust to a new reality.

The remedy isn't to long for yesterday. It is to go where the action is. And salespeople, being opportunistic by nature, and gregarious, are well positioned to detect where things are heading.

Instead of telling yourself bad times or sales reversals are personal, pervasive, and permanent, actively and deliberately repeat the opposite, as a constructive affirmation.

Tell yourself your misses and unearned deals (1) Aren't my fault; (2) Aren't happening everywhere to everyone; and (3) These problems will pass. If they don't I'll quickly abandon what I'm doing and find something to sell that is more productive and more in demand.

One way or another, you can control your self-talk. When you do you'll stay positive and succeed more often. Figure out what works for you, whether that involves ice swimming or something else!

14

Meta Ways to Build Trust

Buyers need to trust us, unless they are so familiar with a brand of finished goods that we're selling which literally sells itself.

I don't need to find they guy at 7-11 to be credible and believable if I'm popping in to buy a Diet Coke. His Coke is going to be the same as anyone else's. So, trust is irrelevant, unless he is so marginal that I believe he's selling bootlegged Coke.

Or, if I suspect his patrons have cleverly tampered with his products, à la Tylenol, I might be concerned. But really, his personal is part of the sale, but in a simple transaction, usually it's minor.

But if we're selling services that take considerable know-how and ability to deliver, as I do, then we must signal to prospects that we're capable.

Doing this can be straightforward, but there are some traps.

For instance, there is the Shakespearean conundrum. We want to arouse a sense of trust, so prospects will let us do our thing and cooperate. If they're jittery about us, they'll intrude, and want reassurances that we're doing as planned and all is okay.

Assurances take time to make, and it's a pain to be doubted.

But here's the conundrum. If we spend too much time and energy saying, you can trust me, everything will be fine, there's nothing to worry about, don't worry— we won't fail, then we may be "protesting too much," as Shakespeare once described it.

Those really good at something seldom have to crow about their accomplishments. Yet at the same time, if we pay no heed to the need for people to feel they can trust us, this will be an open question, and like an open wound, it could fester, until treated properly.

When I'm doing original, customized training and development programs, involving hundreds of managers and front line personnel, this can take up to a year to put into place and make fully operational.

And sometimes, we aren't achieving visible results for several weeks. So, with the resulting suspense, my contacts can become, for lack of a better term, paranoid.

Some have career capital on the line. They may have brought me into their companies. If I succeed, so do they.

So, how can I assure them all will be well, and yet not over-sell the idea so they come to doubt its veracity?

I came up with this meta-communication:

What we do works™

This is an utterly brief, inescapably understandable way of saying I have the authority of results.

You can also extrapolate these sub-messages that this line carries with it:

Trust the process.

I've done this a lot.

I'm a reliable professional.

And of course, if you come to doubt what I'm saying and doing:

Stay the course!

It took considerable time and effort to craft "What we do works™."

But once I had, it was like open sesame to creating instant understanding and cooperation. I coined the phrase in Houston, Texas at a mutual fund company.

They gave me carte blanche to improve their 200-strong and struggling customer service folks. I developed something brand new, a conversational path that produced shorter and better conversations. I also created some special metrics, called TEAMeasures™.

These innovations were folded into new seminars, one for front line reps and 1 for managers.

By the time we reached the conclusion of my work, that company leapt from #24 out of a field of 26 peer group companies to number 4. The following year, utilizing my special methods, they rose to #1 and stayed there for a dozen years.

So, my claim to effectiveness is definitely grounded in results. But how could I sum this up, especially when selling the program to other companies?

That's where having this pithy slogan came in handy. In fact, it was so memorable, that I had clients telling other people, "What he does works!"

Even they found this simple to remember and recite, a genuine communication shortcut.

And above all, it is a true meta-communication. It says, buckle up and enjoy the ride. I've been down this road several times and I know it, perfectly.

Did I mention it has the virtue of being short? I love this part.

I'm a true believer in the idea that if you really know what you're talking about you can express it concisely. One of my best-selling audio programs and seminars is "Crystal Clear Communication."

In it, I emphasize this point. Anything you can do to cut out the fluff, the extra words, the confusing and the convoluted, is well worth the effort.

Plus, there is a perception in buyers that the more direct and succinct you are, the greater the odds are that you're telling the truth.

Sometimes this can take the form of making a bold claim. I did this with the title of my best-selling book, You Can Sell Anything By Telephone!

At the time I wrote it I was doing seminars across the country. And one of the most frequently asked questions was, "Can you sell THIS by phone."

Once, legendary Silicon Valley entrepreneur, Andy Grove, of Intel, called me and asked the very same question. "Can you sell processors by phone?"

When I was jogging, my title popped into mind, answering all of these piecemeal questions with the blanket statement, yes you can!

That title energized my writing and as I was banging out the manuscript I distinctly recall thinking, this is going to be a bestseller!

It became one, I believe in large part because that title was so bold and conclusive that it threw down the gauntlet to any doubters.

So, how can YOU come up with these snappy meta communications, phrases and slogans and headlines that signal value to prospects?

First, consider this: There is almost always a better, shorter, punchier way of articulating a thought, a benefit, or a claim. Consider what I may have started with before I got to what we do works.

We've had great success helping companies to improve their sales and service. We've trained thousands of people in Fortune 500 companies and in smaller firms and star-ups. This has given us a strong track record that you can count on in selecting us.

It's true, but wordy.

There was a famous communication experiment done and then replicated. A control group was given a letter to read and then a test to take on its contents.

Let's say they scored an 85% on the test.

An experimental group was given the same letter. But in their case, every other word was blacked-out, making the letter, literally half-readable.

We would think that their score on the comprehension test might be half of the control group's. If control averaged 85%, then with half the letter to go on, the experimental group would score around 42-43%, right?

Maybe, if they were lucky, they'd get half the answers right.

What in fact happened is the group with half a letter outperformed all expectations. Instead of scoring half as well, they scored at about 85% of the control group's rate.

How could they achieve such high scores after suffering such a handicap?

As it turned out, not having the other half of the letter wasn't nearly as detrimental for a very significant reason.

Language is redundant. We repeat ourselves. Over and over again.

For fun, I just did what I'm describing. I said language is redundant. Meaning, it's repetitious. Golly, I just did it AGAIN!

I said three times what I could have said only once. So, if you're trying to come up with shorter and better ways of formulating features, benefits, slogans, headlines, and titles, you can probably X-out half of what you initially write down on a page.

For instance, in this very last paragraph, I inserted a typical redundancy that could be easily eliminated. Note the very last sentence.

You can probably X-out half of what you initially write down on a page.

"Write down" is a conventional phrase, but do I really need to use both words. Wouldn't "write" suffice?

While we're at it, let's examine the beginning of the sentence. Does the word, "probably" add any special value? Probably, not!

X-out that word, too.

The next step is to substitute smaller words for big ones.

"What we do works" contains one-syllable words. Each word is in common usage, so you would be looking far and wide for an English speaker who does not immediately understand what I mean.

You've heard the old adage about communicating: say what you mean, and mean what you say. That's just as powerful as what we do works.

Say what you mean and mean what you say is mono-syllabic, all one syllable words. (Oops, there's another redundancy I could eliminate.)

Heroes are often depicted in movies as people "of few words." Cut down on the number you use, and you'll often boost your credibility and clout.

A famous commentator once apologized to a correspondent. "I'm sorry this is so lengthy. If I had more time, I would have made it shorter."

This wise meta-communication underscores what I'm saying. Take the time to abbreviate and improve your messages. Typically, they'll become both shorter and better while promoting greater trust in you.

15

"Are You Trying To Sell Me Something?"

If you ever want a clear confirmation of the power of Meta Selling to change channels of communication, consider what customers do to us when they abruptly ask:

"Are you trying to SELL me something?"

With this query, they're stopping the show, so to speak.

First, you can't ignore this blurt and carry on as if nothing happened. If you tried, you'd be acting rudely.

Second, there is an obvious Meta component to the challenge. They're trying to get you to comment on what you're doing. They know, if they succeed, you'll have to stop what you're doing in order to comment on what you're doing.

Now, the fun begins. How can you reply, retaining your composure, and marching undeterred toward your persuasive goal?

If you say, "No," you could be lying. In short order, even if the prospect listens to you she'll figure out you're not truthful and your cause will fail.

If you say, "Yes!" you may fare no better, except you can feel good that you've disallowed the shaming inherent in the question. You see, "Are you selling something?" makes selling sound dirty, nasty, and uncalled for.

Admitting to it is cause for embarrassment or loss of face if you believe the negative associations people imbue selling with. Also, there is a sense among salespeople that their techniques should be stealthy or invisible to buyers.

If you are doing your job correctly, you don't suffer from what one wise sales manager termed, "Sales Breath." For instance, Sales Breath is telegraphing your persuasive intent by seeming too enthusiastic with no apparent reason, too early in the encounter.

"Great, wonderful, perfect!" are specific words that can cast a foul pall over the proceedings as fast as turned-off prospects can say goodbye.

Sales Breath is also a meta-communication, an inadvertent and deal-killing one.

Sellers, realizing the antipathy engendered through their Sales Breath try to do the impossible. They try to stop breathing.

Figuratively speaking, they abandon their classical sales tools because they're afraid they'll turn-off buyers. And some savvy buyers, some of whom are sellers themselves with equal or even superior sales training to ours, will be able to detect and call us on the techniques we deploy.

I've had some prospects interject things such as, "Good appeal to urgency!" and "Nice close!"

Sometimes these are inside jokes, ways of winking at us as we do our thing, which may evidence a sense of admiration on their part.

"Hey, you're not bad at this!" they're meta-communicating.

Generally, this kind of interruption is also a show-stopper, just as the "Are you trying to sell me something?" is.

How can we sell while narrating our techniques at the same time?

From a practical standpoint, you have to ask yourself, if this person is insistent on giving me a rough time, should I persist, anyway?

I don't think it's worth the effort.

After they've signaled their intent to obstruct your flow, you're on notice that making the sale will be a tough slog, at best. It will consume time and extra effort.

You probably won't get the deal when the dust settles, and you may even dislike yourself for trying and especially for wasting your breath even if it seemed like Sales Breath!

I got to the point, when I was cold calling that I would offer a snappy rejoinder when asked, "Are you selling me something?"

"If I succeed, YES!"

"Well, well, well," they'd sputter, and I'd let them go by sincerely saying, "Well, thank you for your courtesy!"

They'd be left thinking, "What's he talking about? I wasn't courteous!"

Here's a comment on that rejoinder of mine. I said thank you. I seemed to deliver a compliment, unearned, but a compliment, nonetheless.

My tone stair-stepped. "Courtesy" went way up, signaling sincerity and enthusiasm.

Now this is supremely important: I left the encounter on a high note!

This reduces the proclivity to ruminate on sales conversations that sour and to obsess over being mistreated.

More significant than earning any given sale is preserving my desire to push for the next one. I have to be at cause, and not at effect. My chi, my life force needs to flow strongly.

By shaming me into believing I'm doing something immoral or undesirable, that one nasty prospect can dam up my flow, dropping big boulders into my sales stream.

We can't let that happen.

Early in my selling career, one of my trainers declared: "Nothing happens in our economy without selling!"

He went on to say if selling were to disappear, of course our jobs would go away.

He also said in the gravest imaginable voice: Nothing sells itself. People need to be persuaded, and that's our job.

If there is a circumstance where items fly off of shelves, like the latest Christmas toy for kids, then companies only need clerks, not sellers.

Order takers can be hired at the lowest wages, not order makers, who actively get people to buy what they would not have bought, at least with the same speed or the same price, if our exertions were not brought to bear upon them.

A good salesperson will never be out of work for very long!

These notions are worth repeating because they still apply today, perhaps more than ever.

What has changed is the sophistication of some buyers. Frankly, they're more educated, if only in some practical habits such as not making snap decisions.

The have fairly sophisticated BS monitors, as one of my Xerox clients termed their defenses against sales puffery. They're quick to deflate the air from exaggerations and unsupported assertions.

And it is the fact that we're dealing with what communication theorist Wilbur Schramm once called, "The Obstinate Audience," that requires us to expand our Meta Selling repertoire of techniques.

"Are you trying to sell me something?" is a great challenge to which to apply Meta Sales principles.

What are some other possible replies, ones that open a new channel, that shit the tone from attack-and-defense to something more amiable and useful?

Let's throw out a few for your consideration:

"Not if it isn't right for you. I have a quick question that will tell us if it is . . ."

Then you ask the question without seeking additional permission. If you get a reply that affirms the benefit in carrying on the encounter, then do so, without apology and without abandoning any of the content you need to cover.

What if people say, "I'm really busy!"

"So am I. I'll make it brief."

Then, carry on as if the interruption never occurred.

The interesting meta-message you're sending is, "I'm just like you are, not a time waster, so be assured I'll cut to the chase."

Do you?

Do you in any way shrink the needed information you need to convey?

No!

But you said you'd make it brief. Well, you always make it as brief as you can. They don't know how long it was before, so you're not violating any expectations.

"Will this take long?" some will ask. Use a similar reply, "No, I'll make it brief."

This reminds me of what I sometimes say to reticent seminar participants, especially if they've been involuntarily assigned to my program.

"As you might imagine, I've covered this material a number of times. And it's always more fun and a good learning experience if you have questions and comments and I can customize the program to meet your needs. But if you'd prefer not to talk, don't worry, I won't call on you or embarrass you. I have plenty of material to cover during our time together so sit back and enjoy the ride!"

This is a meta-message that says, "Be you." You can relax. I'm confident in what I'm bringing to you and frankly you don't have to do anything you don't want to do.

You can see smiles lighting up dark faces, and actually hear people exhale.

Recently, I customized a training program for an international company. The day before the first session, one of my contacts called me.

I could tell he was nervous because some of his career capital was riding on the program. It was he who recommended bringing me in.

So, I meta-communicated:

"I'm all set and looking forward to it. We're going to have a lot of fun!"

And we did. I prepared perfectly, and the group was ready to have a good time and cover material that could help them to negotiate their sales pricing.

Putting people at ease is usually accomplished through meta-communication.

This is why sellers have told jokes. When people laugh, their endorphins flow, making them feel good.

What else can we say when asked, "Are you trying to sell me something?"

"Gee, I never thought of that. Would you like to buy something?"

Yes, this is smartass. But think of the pluses.

It may make the person laugh the laugh of self-recognition. It's way too early in the encounter to sell OR to buy is what this response is saying.

Naturally, you'll elicit a "No!" which isn't surprising. But you can instantly follow that with:

"Of course you don't, and that's only right. I haven't said anything, yet!"

Then you might be able to continue, especially if the person gets the joke.

"The reason I'm calling on you is . . ."

16

I Have A Little Problem On My Hands & Was Hoping You Could Help Me Out

There are meta sales presentations that have built entire industries.

In the office supply business, the mis-shipment pitch is one of them.

"Hello, this is Gary Goodman with All Flakes Federal Supply. What's the name of the owner there, please?

"Bill-can I speak to him please? I'll be happy to hold, thanks."

"Uh, this is Bill."

"Hi Bill, this is Gary Goodman with All Flakes Federal Supply. We don't know each other, but I have a little problem on my hands and I was hoping you might be able to help me out."

"Well, okay, I will if I can!"

"Thanks. I'm in the office supply business here in Phoenix, and recently I shipped a small order of Bic ballpoint pens to a client in your area. I just learned he's gone bankrupt. If he gets the order, I'm toast. If I can reroute those pens to you, I can save you a lot of money.

"How much are they?"

"Well I sent him two small boxes, each has a two gross of pens. These are the Bic PF-49s. They sell for 49 cents each, they're marked 49 on the barrel. If you can handle them I'll get them into you at only 33 cents each, delivered."

"How many are there?"

"Only 2 gross to the box, that's 288 pens in each box. That runs only \$_____ per box, DELIVERED, okay?"

"Gee, I don't think I can do that many."

"Well, between using them and losing them, you'd be surprised. How many waiters do you have there at the Embers Café?"

"About 15."

"They're going to go through a pen a week, easily. That's 70 pens a month, so it's about an 8-month supply for you. And they have a shelf life of 3 years, so you can't go wrong. Can you help me out?"

"Can I take just one box?"

"Yeah I can do that, and it WILL help. I show your address as: Is that right? Okay, great, you can expect those to reach you by, I would say, Tuesday or so, Okay? You saved my life on this, Bill. Thanks so much!"

There's a lot going on in this presentation. I'm going to ask you to put aside your concerns about the questionable nature of the mis-shipment story. If you don't, you'll miss the deep power of this pitch, which has general applicability and really highlights some important Me Selling precepts.

Let's take these Meta Selling gambits in order.

It would be a mistake to think this presentation begins when Bill comes onto the line. Getting him to answer the call is really the first sale. I call getting through administrative screening, "The sales before the sale."

Think of it as Sale #1. Without it, you'll never get to Bill, Sale #2.

I start with: "Hello, this is Gary Goodman with All Flakes Federal Supply. What's the name of the owner there, please?

Note, I didn't just ask, "What's the name of the owner there, please?" If I did, I'd sound more threatening, sending a meta message that I'm definitely a stranger.

By first disclosing my name and company, I'm sending a signal saying I'm a straight-up businessperson. I become transparent. That induces trust.

We know from psychological research that self-disclosure arouses trust, so I'm tapping into this truth.

We also know that there's an unwritten rule about what happens when we disclose, especially if we're the first to do it in a transaction. That act encourages reciprocity.

If we were at a business mixer, and I walked up and said, "I'm Gary Goodman. I'm in the sales raining business. What do you do?" I'd probably get a suitable reply.

Contrast that with NOT disclosing first. If I just asked, "What do you do?" I might engender anxiety, instead of a comfy reply.

Back to screening: By becoming "visible" in volunteering who I am and my company name, I'm sending a silent meta message that I should be treated with respect and I "belong" in the conversation.

Have you ever watched a stray dog running through a neighborhood? It scurries, making nervous, darting glances in all directions. It's signaling its insecurities and drawing to itself the hostility of other dogs in the neighborhood as well as people.

By disclosing, I'm saying this call IS my territory. Again. I'm here because I belong here.

So, right away, with subtlety, I have differentiated myself from typical salespeople and from those that want something for nothing. I GAVE something, first, by giving my name and affiliation.

I can't overstate the importance of this. Moreover, volunteering information right away starts a sequence of give-and-take communicating that makes screeners respond to me, instead of setting me up to respond to them, and their 20 questions.

(There's a more thorough example from a hugely successful program I designed for Xerox Computer Services, which I'll share in a few minutes. It will dramatize the effectiveness of re-scripting the entire screening sequence based on Meta Selling principles.)

Let's go back to ballpoint pens. When Bill comes onto the line, what do I say?

"Hi Bill, this is Gary Goodman with All Flakes Federal Supply. We don't know each other, but I have a little problem on my hands and I was hoping you might be able to help me out."

I use his name. Names are music to our ears. If I say his with fondness, respect, authority, or a combination of these elements, I'll get his attention and score points right away.

But here's comes the Meta Selling marvels:

"We don't know each other, but I have a little problem on my hands and I was hoping you might be able to help me out."

Flat-out, I acknowledge we're strangers. You could think such a disclosure would widen any gap between us. If this is a cold call, we just jumped from the fridge to the freezer, right?

Not so, it does the opposite. A frank disclosure is endearing in this context. It shows vulnerability, which sets up the next part of the statement:

". . . but I have a little problem on my hands and I was hoping you might be able to help me out."

The meta message I'm sending is "I have no right to ask you for a favor." Yet this is precisely what a person of good manners will feel like doing, when approached this way.

We like doing what we think we have all rights not to do. It makes us feel autonomous, and in this circumstance, noble and generous.

Indeed, saying to someone, "I have no right to ask you this," is a very powerful way of asking permission to ask for something you have no right to receive!

Compare this to coming from a "You owe me this" or an entitlement position. It could be true, that someone is in your debt. But being reminded of it the wrong way makes us feel we're acting under compulsion, and we often reject such demands.

There are some other powerful elements operating in the presentation as a whole that are worth pointing out.

We've just appealed to someone's higher motives, but we're also going to appeal to their self-interest. By solving "my problem" they're going to save a considerable amount of money.'

So, they can feel noble and business savvy at the same time.

The mis-shipment pitch contains two essential elements of encouraging fast, almost reflexive approvals of your proposals: Urgency and scarcity.

If that shipment of pens reaches the person that just declared bankruptcy, then all is lost. The wheels of the delivery truck are spinning, getting those two small boxes ever closer to becoming a total financial loss for the seller.

Can't you just see the last grains of sand falling to the bottom of the hourglass? Time is running out?

It is said that urgency and scarcity are needed to sell almost everything, and here's why:

People think they have forever to make a decision, so they delay in making them. The objection or stall, "Not now; maybe later" is one of the top ways prospects weal out of making commitments.

One of the most popular TV shows of recent vintage is "24," starring Keifer Sutherland. The premise of the original series is one hour of show time is equal to one hour of the reality being depicted in the drama.

By putting the entire season of shows on a 24 hour clock, this dramatic device added urgency and scarcity to the proceedings." The events became riveting, and you didn't want to miss a minute of it.

I took a screenwriting class, and "The Ticking Clock" is one of the most popular formulas for creating tension and sustaining interest.

I know a fellow in the advertising specialties business that uses this ploy to perfection.

He imprints the name of contractors and plumbers on stickers that affix to tape measures. He tells his buyers that they can sell the items or give them away as "thank you's" to their customers. By having their names and phone numbers and web sites on the sticker, this reminds people to do business with them.

To overcome the tendency to procrastinate, the ad specialty seller says, "we have a container of these tape measures coming into port next week. We've already sold out 70% of the shipment. Order now, and you'll save 22% because that's what the next container is going to cost, if you wait."

What he does, on a regular schedule is send emails saying, "80% of the container is sold," and then "85% is sold," and then, "93% is sold."

You get the idea. By using a countdown to zero, and he WILL get to zero, and tell them so, he is authenticating his scarcity claim. He wants them to feel they lost out on something.

But then he'll go back and say, "I do have a container coming in of LED flashlights that we can print your name on. I have only X number available, Can you use them?"

If his last countdown campaign created the right sense of a lost opportunity, then his prospects will be inclined to grab the next offer, fearing they'll lose out there, as well.

Urgency and scarcity sell well.

Just for a moment, I want to reflect on something, which I find very interesting. Stationery stores and bigger discounters, like Office Max and Office Depot are lucky to sell one or two pens, or at most a dozen to each customer that is in the market for writing instruments.

Phone rooms came along that sniffed an opportunity. Why sell one dozen when you can sell two boxes of pens with 12 dozen in each? In other words, why sell 12 items at a shot when you can sell 576?

The business "problem" retailers face is that they are always there, open from 9 to 9, right? If I want some pens, I can buy them 12 hours a day, six or seven days a week.

Why rush?

The minute they put a banner in the window that I see that says: "Lost our lease: Everything 90% off!" then I just have to pull into the lot and have a look.

That'

That's urgency and scarcity at work, and almost always, it works.

Just one more thing about these twin motivations before we conclude this segment. There are two kinds or urgency: Internal and external. Let's say we're having a Memorial Day sale where everything is marked down 25%.

Is that internal or external? We decide when we're having a sale, and that's an internal decision. But by pegging it to Memorial Day, we're making it external, obeying the rules of the clock, which limits the sale to 3 days.

The general rule is external urgency is more credible. By saying the next tape measure shipment would cost more, who is to blame? Not the retailer, because it's out of his control, right?

If he seems to be manipulating the price, in total charge of it, then his offer will lack the same credibility and effectiveness.

Smartly making your problem their problem is a shortcut to fast sales.

17

Do You Sincerely Want to be RICH?

A pioneer in the mutual fund business, Bernie Cornfeld, earned immortality in the annals of selling with this daring and succinct come-on to investors:

Do You Sincerely Want to be RICH?

Later, a biography of his life would be penned, using this challenge as its title.

What Cornfeld was boldly doing in a way few had done before is qualifying prospects. Essentially, his overture to potential buyers is a qualifying question.

The concept of doing this is essential in selling and it boils down to this rationale. Time is limited. If we squander ours by chatting up the wrong folks, we'll starve. Qualifying questions separate the serious from the frivolous.

Thus much effort is directed at puzzling over who is most likely to buy from a given universe of suspects. Typically, we set our sights on those that have certain promising characteristics.

Amazon does this algorithmically. At the beginning of summer I bought a major league baseball hat at a great price. I scanned another team's chapeaus but they were too pricey, given how hard I am on them with jogging at the beach and tennis.

Now that summer is whispering its last, Amazon is teasing me with far better offers on that second hat. Why not? I'm a qualified buyer, and everybody knows the best prospects are typically those that have bought before.

Well, this is low hanging fruit for Amazon because they track my purchases and make bets on what I'll also be interested in. If we're selling to strangers, and we don't have any real feeling for their predisposition to buy, we need to be more forthcoming and ask them, directly.

What are we qualifying them for?

Do they have the means to buy, the money? An otherwise rich company that operates on strict budgets may have the means but not the authorization to purchase.

So, authority, decision-making power enters the equation. The higher up we move in organizations the more power our contacts have to make out-of-budget buys.

What Cornfeld taps with his brilliant question is the motivation to buy. Do you sincerely WANT to be rich, he asks.

This drive to buy may top everything else. We're aware of the expression, "Where there's a will, there's a lawyer."

Just kidding, that expression says, "Where there's a will, there's a way."

Perhaps the opposite of this proposition is even more powerful. If people don't want to buy, practically nothing will make them do it.

Legendary ballplayer and quipster Yogi Berra said it this way: "If people don't want to come out to the ball-park, nobody's gonna stop 'em."

In theory, a smart seller wants to hear prospect signal their intentions to buy in this order: Yes, No, Maybe.

If we outright ask them, "Are you going to buy something?" we most want to hear a yes, for obvious reasons.

Secondly, we want a firm no, if they're genuinely not coming to the ballpark.

With a "no" we can save our breath and get onto the important business of selling that seat to real fan. Once the game starts, it's too late and we suffer a total loss.

Finally, if our heads are on straight, we'll reluctantly accept a "maybe." I say if our heads are on straight because maybes are usually time wasters.

The lukewarm prospect doesn't really know what he wants, so he hems and haws and stalls. This forces us into an endless follow-up loop.

"Are we ready to move forward?" we ask, hopefully.

"Well, I don't know. Give me another week or so, okay?"

This can go on forever.

Even if we eventually close a maybe, and get the deal, our cost in sunken time and effort and in missed opportunities could vastly exceed our commissions and profits from earning that deal.

Qualifying can provide us a glimpse into the future. It addresses this crystal ball question, "If I invest time with you, will it pay off?

In a sense, as you repeat this question out loud, you can hear how strange it is. Are people ever 100% certain about what actions they are going to take?

The future is iffy, for everybody, so in a sense, it is unfair to get people to predict whether they'll buy from us. They may not like us, or to get turned off by our prices.

Still, we crave clues. Yeah, the future is all kinds of mysterious, but let's cut through that.

Are we heading toward a deal, here?

This is called, taking someone's temperature. Are they hot or cold? Warming up or are they heading in the other direction?

Inquiring minds want to know!

I read a *Los Angeles Times* article the other day. The journalist received a call from a source that said the scribe was the inheritor of many millions of dollars. He simply had to authenticate who he is.

Inasmuch as the writer is that paper's consumer watchdog, he instantly thought this was an identity-theft scam. They'd get his vital information and off they'd go.

But no, this was a longer con. To learn about them he went along with the game, posing as a good victim. They sent him official looking certificates, but when the time came, they asked him to advance some money so his new fortune could be forwarded to him.

Of course, he declined, and wrote an article, instead.

Take the scam part out of this story, and the journalist is the prospect from hell. He plays along, even feigning interest, extending the conversations, while consuming our time. In reality, he never really intends to buy.

There are prospects that don't realize they are full of bull. It is a secret that they keep, even from themselves. In the sales trade they're called tire-kickers and looky-loos.

"Please don't take offense, but are you ever going to buy?"

This sounds like a rude question, but at a certain point, it becomes fair game. Clearly, it is a meta-message that says:

"For a typical transaction like this, we're surely taking an extraordinary amount of time, aren't we?

And that is another meta-question we can ask. What is the worst thing they can do? Say no to our offer? Remember the order of what savvy sellers seek: A yes, a no, and finally, a maybe.

Advancing from a maybe to a no is actually making progress!

Today's companies use enterprise software and lead tracking programs. Our prospects are cued up for us to call. And when calls are finished we're required to make note about what was said and follow-up dates and times.

Some companies badger sales reps to continue phoning prospects eight or more times, after an initial attempt is made. There is a presumption this relentless process operates from.

Prospects become more sellable with increased numbers of contacts.

Well, if they're avoiding your outreach, which becomes obvious after you have left two or more messages, then I doubt they are becoming more sales-friendly.

They're more likely sending a meta-message of their own:

Don't chase me. I'm hiding.

Think of it like dating. If they're ghosting you, making themselves impossible to reach, they may be madly in love: But not with you.

Move on! Let them go! Turn the page!

You can even comfort yourself, concluding it's about THEM; not me."

My problem with those software programs that force us into making an arbitrary number of follow-ups is that they substitute a statistical fiction for our intuition.

If you think they're messing with you, through silence or through mock participation, you're probably right. But even if you're technically wrong, if you BELIEVE they're messing with you, and you've developed some defensiveness as a result, you're right. They ARE messing with you because they've gotten into your head.

The same prescription applies: Move on! Let them go! Turn the page!

Let's focus for a minute on how far I'll go to qualify people. Imagine you've contacted someone and they ask, "Can you send me something about that?"

That sounds promising, yes? Interested folks crave more information. So, if you rush off the line and email them your standard packet with a tiny bit of customizing, that would be expected.

But it doesn't end with that. In all likelihood, you'll need to follow up that email with another call. You'll leave a voice mail. You'll call again, and leave yet another voice mail.

That initial request to "send me something" spawns a huge number of subsequent investments requiring your time and effort.

And I have news for you. We assumed the request for info was a positive thing, a buying signal. But it could have been the opposite, a convenient way for that person to get you off the line.

By feigning interest, they spared themselves the pain of rejecting you, forthrightly, while they probably believe they helped you to save face by not being overtly rejected.

But that short-term pleasure becomes long-term pain because we failed to qualify their interest BEFORE sending out the information.

Here's how I do it:

Sure, I'll be happy to send you an email. It will contain X, Y, and Z. And I'll follow-up with you tomorrow about this time, so we can move forward, okay?"

If they cut me off before I can tell them what will be in the info, then they're unqualified. They're simply getting me off the line.

In all likelihood, I won't waste my time sending them anything because I know doing it will set me up to make numerous follow-up attempts, probably for nothing.

Note in my telephonic send-off I try to set up a follow-up date and time. This says I'm sending the info with the understanding that it will lead to another conversation.

I'm not going to rely on the info to do my closing for me.

I even say I'll follow-it up "so we can move forward, okay?"

In other words, sending information out is not an idle exercise.

If I have had a good conversation with someone who then becomes a ghost, I'll leave this voice message:

"Hi, this is Gary Goodman. We spoke the other day and if you'll kindly give me a heads-up about what you'd like to do I'd appreciate that. I can be reached by text or phone at 818-970-GARY, which is 818-970-4279, or by email at gary@customersatisfaction.com. And if you'd simply say yes, no, or maybe, that would be great, Thanks."

This has worked very well for me. Recently, one potential seminar sponsor replied by email with a no, that he wouldn't consider moving forward for another year.

Well, forget about that guy. That's a no, but it's worthwhile because it says spend zero effort with him.

Another sponsor replied with what I would call a legitimate maybe. He said he needs 90 days of lead-time to schedule any event. We were at about 50 days at that point. Also, he mentioned he wanted to see how my event fared with a kindred sponsor who was already scheduled.

Both of these replies were quick and reasonably clear. That's what we want from effective qualification.

It's worth commenting on the fact that I'm giving three choices for their reply: yes, no, or maybe.

I don't really want a maybe, unless it is authentic. They may need time to run the idea past other people, to get approval, and so on. That's legit.

I'm also saying it's okay to say no. This is very powerful as a meta-message. The way our business communication game is played, we kill people with kindness, seldom really telling them where they stand.

Jack Welch, former CEO of General Electric says this indirectness is an organizational disease. Without a doubt, it wastes an amazing amount of productivity, and not just the seller's.

Buyers suffer evasion costs, that aren't apparent to them.

It takes time and effort to listen to a seller's never-ending voice mails. It wears on us to know we are contributing to a seller's delusion that she may be pursuing a legitimate deal where there is none to be had.

If sellers are made to be more inefficient, these costs must be passed on to the buyer in the form of higher prices or less service tendered when they do buy.

Even if I never intend to buy a door-to-door vacuum cleaner salesperson's product, by making him less efficient, I suffer the cost of his lost productivity. He earns less and pays less in taxes. This means worse schools, roads, and public safety for me and for my family.

His company has less profit that it can create jobs with, and that might mean one less entry level post is available to my kids, or to my neighbor's relatives.

"What goes around comes around" is an apt description of the inefficiencies caused when ineffective prospect qualifying is done, along with the worsened sales results it garners.

I've gone so far as to say this to prospects. I'll explicitly say:

Saving my time is going to save you money. So please get back to me on this at your earliest.

In fairness to prospects, sellers can be too quick to disqualify prospects. We can ask too much of them too soon.

As a check against this, we can meta-communicate:

Do you feel you have enough information with which to make a decision on this?

What factor will be of primary importance to you as you evaluate this?

Do you feel we're delivering on that?

Qualifying buyers is an imperfect art. Sometimes it backfires, evoking a premature rejection. But more times than not, it saves you time and money.

And that's a huge plus. If you sincerely want to be rich, do this well!

18

Smart Calls Versus Dumb Calls

"There's one thing about selling that's different than any other career," my mentor at Time-Life Books intoned with unusual gravity. "If you're good at it, you'll never be out of work for very long. The world will always need salesmen."

This brings a smile to my lips for a few reasons. Retail selling constitutes one of the biggest parts of the economy that still employs salespeople. But as you know, retail selling like retailing, itself is under siege from online sources such as Amazon.

Record numbers of stores have been shuttered during the last decade. There are some survivors at this point that are bucking the trend, notably Nordstrom and Target. But they are, indeed, unusual.

So, sellers, along with shelf stockers and cashiers are being put out of work. Moreover, those of us that do direct selling, outside of retail, smirk when we see those words put together, retail + selling.

Clerks are order-takers, not order makers. Typically, there is very little persuasion involved in their jobs. Someone that picks up the phone to sell newspaper ad space to a retailer is actually getting that prospect to select and prefer that company and medium over radio, TV, pay-per click, social media and other channels.

The sales retail clerks facilitate can often be done by robots, which are already on the scene in the form of self-checkout terminals that we use, and in many cases favor, because the lines are shorter.

Ironically, I select self-checkout over real humans for another reason. I want to be spared the happy talk current clerks have been trained to use.

"And how is your day?" is not a question that will induce me to come back. Worse, "Did you find everything you were looking for?" is an invitation to useless chatter that will not instantly put into my hands something that wasn't on the shelf.

If you reply "no," that could stop the line you're in, causing you embarrassment for wasting people's time, and eventuating in a bagger making an idle trip to a shelf to verify the absence of the item.

"Sorry!" is the weak result of this sequence.

Thus, when selling, or more to the point, customer service is offered in much of today's retailing, it is not an integral part of the transaction but a belated add-on that delivers a minus in the overall experience.

No wonder automation and online shopping are reducing the ranks of retail "sales" staffs. They aren't much good when they are present.

But there is another reason I smile when I think of Larry's dramatic statement that a good seller will never be out of work, for long.

What we used to think of as good sales jobs are disappearing, fast. These are full-time opportunities that yield significantly above-average wages for a moderate amount of work.

In actual money terms, they deliver to doers at least $100,000.00 per year, or $8,333.33 per month. That's not rock star money, and a decent software developer in Silicon Valley makes far more.

But in a pinch, it can keep the wolf from the door. Add-in even a high-deductible health plan and a 401K that the employer contributes to, and it is "okay work."

If you can find it, that is. Since the Great Recession of 2008, these sorts of sales jobs have been disappearing from the scene. I track sales jobs closely because it is from help-wanted ads that I gauge whether certain prospects for my sales training are growing and thus constitute good leads for me.

I've noticed several trends.

The days have passed when companies offered compensation plans that were heavy on salary and relatively light on commissions. I'd peg the old format as roughly a 75%-25% ratio. If you were an exceptional seller, you might achieve bonuses on top of salary + commission, or a higher base salary to reflect your superior achievement.

But you'd still be mostly a "salaryman," as the Japanese have referred to their corporate workers.

Today, the amount of guaranteed to variable pay has been reversed.

It's not unusual to find jobs that pay $30,000.00 a year as a fixed sum, and then commissions are paid against that number, or on top of it.

While companies boast that you can earn six-figures, $100,000.0000 and up, it's pretty much a lie. There may be one or two "show horses" on the team that reportedly earn the bigger money, but when you inquire about them, typically they've been around for years.

And they are the recipients of favored treatment. Though this sounds like a lament out of the play and movie, "Glengarry Glen Ross," the real insiders get more leads and better leads.

A salesman I know worked for a business opportunities outfit that paid a tiny salary but offered a significant performance incentive. Steve was experienced, and he sprinted toward the top of the chart right away.

In fact, he was the only person that gave Tony, the top dog, any competition. After being there for about seven months, Steve and Tony were running neck and neck for the top bonus.

By Steve's calculation, because he earned a double-sale in the waning moments of the business year, before Christmas break, he won the contest, and a several-thousand dollar prize.

They came back from break, after New Years, and it was announced Tony had won because a phantom sale in his favor had not been properly logged.

Clearly, this was a rigged result, felt Steve. This treatment was confirmed when the sales manager Lucy, inadvertently blurted out at a meeting that Tony is such a good seller that "We give him twice as many leads as anyone else!"

No wonder how he made the most money and how he always nabbed the highest amount of contest money.

It serves management's purpose to have a show horse such as Tony. "See, he can do it, and so can you!" is the message such a top achiever seems to send. But scratch the surface and you'll often find the game is tilted in his favor.

I'm also seeing some other interesting dynamics in the salesperson personnel marketplace. There is a stratification of the sales job universe into (1) lead generators and (2) closers.

This two-stepped approach has always been around in certain companies. This is especially so, where you find infrequent, large sales bearing huge commissions instead of smaller, more frequent ones.

Business brokerage comes to mind. In this field, you are looking for businesspeople that want to sell their enterprises. It is a needles-in-haystacks hunt that bores most experienced, professional sellers. One could invest a week or two just to find someone that responds "maybe" to the question, "Are you considering selling your business in the next few years?"

Yet that one lead could turn into a half-million dollar deal on the sale of what is considered a small, family-owned enterprise.

Closing the deal, getting the contract to sell that business, like a real estate listing, is almost a guarantee of a payday.

Thus, paying minimum wages to people that will "sit on an auto-dialer" that robotically, phones hundreds or thousands of small businesses each day, makes financial sense.

And you don't need more than a clerk, someone to ask that "are you interested in selling your business" question.

Indeed, this is what selling has become in a world governed by automation and software.

It is an industry buttressed by innumerable "dumb calls" that can be made by dumb people at dumb wages.

Like robots on an automotive assembly line the repetitious work is being done more and more by automation. Dialing one number after the next is replaced by software. All of those motions of mentally deciding to call a certain business, then locating the number on a screen, and then manually making the call, and wading though the no-answers and the answering devices, all of these things, are being done by robots.

Selling as a handmade, bespoke process, is being left to those that make what I call, "smart calls."

I'm going to make some of these, today, after I complete the writing of this segment.

I have a project right now that is being co-sponsored by a well-known, international nonprofit organization. It isn't a school, but it does do some consumer and business education.

I have partnered with this entity to offer one of my seminars that I've customized to its clients. It is co-labeled, so it bears the name of the nonprofit that is "Presenting Dr. Gary S. Goodman in a special seminar."

I'm phoning a relative handful of companies from a list of thousands that will receive an invitation via email. These are high-value targets that meet several criteria.

They are regional stalwarts, some of the largest and most profitable firms in the service area of my client. I have selected them because they can easily send several people with various job titles to my program, and they can afford the price tag.

They also have a proven, objectively verified need for the custom content I'm delivering. Above all, there is futurity in contacting them.

If they buy a seat in my seminar, or even if they don't, they might opt to bring me in-house, to deliver customized training to their personnel. Historically, this has yielded a nice income for me.

In all likelihood, they have a dial-by-name phone directory option that I can use to reach multiple functionaries at the firms.

This is what I can tell you so far about this sales project.

I'm calling into the companies and reaching very few people on my initial attempt. This reflects a growing trend. People are barricaded behind voice mail. Also, they have instructed front line personnel to not divulge their emails or direct extensions.

Dumb calls are stopped in their tracks. No way can you penetrate these fortresses and find the right people to pitch, and then actually make presentations to them with auto-dialers.

My task is to find the names of the top executives and to pitch them on the idea of designating certain underlings to send to my program. I've found I don't have good contact names at this point, so part of my task is to seek them out.

Here's what I did with a medical device company the other day. I went to their web site to update what I knew about them. Their founders are still there, but their staff has doubled, to about 250 people.

Historically, units of 100-500 people have been great targets for my expertise. They aren't large enough to house experts of their own to compete with my credibility or my offerings.

But they are complex enough to need and benefit from my sophisticated techniques, especially in sales and customer service.

I went to www.linkedin.com and researched the company, by name. Instantly, I found the names and background information pertaining to about 100 people associated with the firm.

One woman, by her title, seemed to be a good starting place. I phoned the main number and selected dial-by-name. Instead of divulging her name, the prompt said, "Select one for extension 1111."

I had to assume her name spelled that number, and in a second she came onto the line."

"Hello, Marta?"

"Yes."

"Hi, this is Dr. Gary Goodman. I'm going to be conducting a special seminar with X nonprofit and their CEO has asked me to reach out to your company to invite the right people to attend. Who is it that should get this email invitation I have?"

She mentioned the name of her manager, gave me the right spelling, his email, and also verified that his email address format is in universal use at their company. She also agreed to receive an invitation, herself.

If she could think of any other good recipients, I asked her to forward the email I was sending her to them.

Pleasantly, she agreed.

Before long, I had reached out to about a dozen good "suspects," people that might turn out to be good attendees or who could pass along my invitation.

Much like the "live" script I used with Marta, I left substantially the same voice mail message, indicating I'd be following-up the contact with an email to them.

This is what I call "honeycombing" in a sales process. It is reaching out, simultaneously to multiple contacts in the same enterprise with the same offer.

It can produce remarkable results.

I did this with a snail-mailing to companies with over 100 employees in the Los Angeles and San Francisco regions to promote a self-sponsored seminar I was doing.

I didn't have any contact names, so I decided to adopt their mail-rooms as my own private post offices.

I wrote a cover letter that began with the words, "Dear Mail Room Manager." I said to save trees and curtail needless waste I would be most grateful if they would distribute the five flyers I have inserted to the job titles mentioned on the address portion of the pieces.

One piece read "VP Sales" and the next read "VP Customer Service" and another read "VP Human Resources."

I realized from the get-go that many companies didn't have a "Mail Room Manager," but someone at reception or that handled incoming mail would read my outreach.

Then, presuming they bought into my save-the-trees pitch, they'd dutifully distribute, and not trash, my missive. This meant a currently-employed person at the firm would get the mailing piece.

Lists are notoriously out of date, including commercial ones. Easily you can expect a 20% non-delivery result, which of course is wasteful.

By sending to one functionary I save the price of four "stamps." When you're mailing 20,000 pieces instead of 100,000, you're saving a ton of money!

Anyway, this ended up being a successful mailing for me. One manager, which sent people to my public seminar and quite profitably brought me into do a custom training and development program, told me the following story.

"I was sitting at my desk and as I read your brochure, four other people came to me within the hour and handed me their copies!"

It was uttered as if she witnessed a business miracle!

This is honeycombing. And it is smart selling.

It is the future. This is what I want to meta-communicate to you.

Larry was right and wrong. He was almost correct in saying that if you are a good seller you'll always be able to find work.

I would modify this to say you'll always be able to make-work for yourself. You'll find fewer and fewer pre-manufactured "good" sales jobs as time passes.

This is because you'll never be able to make enough dumb calls to make a smart living. Machines and software are eliminating most repetitious aspects of selling. Wages are being crunched-down to match the severely limited contributions many sales jobs of today permit.

Your value-added will be in using your intelligence to optimize the channels that are not totally shut-off from us. You'll do as I do, purposely phoning the wrong, but accessible person in a company to gain intelligence about the identity and pathways to reaching genuine buyers and influencers.

You'll "get in and spread out" in firms, purposely using redundant pitches to several people to gain entry and purchase for your offers.

You'll exploit lists such as those provided at LinkedIn, as I have done and continue to do.

And you'll learn to make voice mail and email, work together, excellent substitutes for having real-time conversations when they are not practical to achieve.

In a word, you'll work in a way that only, or especially a human can work.

I envision a day in the near future where all human selling will be several cuts above the mundane, the repetitious, the perfunctory and easily cloned.

All selling will be Meta Selling!

19

Tones Talk!

Remember getting into trouble with your parents? At some point you'd be called to account for something and you'd explain why you did it.

Your words might have been sufficient, as in "Bobby made me do it!" or "I don't know" or "It seemed okay at the time," but your mom or dad would get even more upset and snarl, "Don't use that tone with me!"

"What tone?" you'd bleat.

"That tone!" they'd repeat.

This was one of our first introductions to the fascinating fact that tones talk. They send messages of their own.

I'm here to tell you a good amount of successful selling is meta- selling through managing one's tones in optimal ways.

The need for this is dramatized when we get into tone trouble, as we did with our folks.

I think the best example is when our tones and our text conflict. This happens accidentally or on purpose when we come across as being sarcastic.

If I ask you, how do I look, having donned some new duds, and you reply, "You look great," that's a compliment, right?

Not so fast. If the word, "great" is elevated into a high pitch or if it is emphasized, you're probably right. It's meant as praise and it feels rewarding.

But if the pitch goes decidedly down on that word, "great," this sends a signal that says: Don't believe my words to be true, believe their opposite.

Here's where it gets tricky. We can and often do sound accidentally sarcastic. Or just short of that, but still negatively, we come across as half-heated and unenthusiastic.

But we don't mean it. We're accidentally torpedoing out words. At best, we come across as lackadaisical, at worst, we sound insincere or purposely self-destructive when we're selling.

Comedians often use sarcasm to get huge laughs. The humor comes exactly from the disconnection between what we are saying on the surface and what the underlying meaning really is.

One person turns to the other and says, "I can't remember the last time we had a romantic evening out, just the two of us."

"I know," replies the other. "Next time we should bring someone else along."

Or, "I can't remember the last time we were romantic."

"How long have you had this memory problem?" responds the other.

Seriously, if we inadvertently use sarcasm in selling, we'll get into trouble. I knew a fellow account executive in the leasing business who was, when he could score gigs, a real-live comedian. He had me in stitches because his cubicle was next to mine.

The problem was he was so used to using sarcasm for fun that it carried over into his selling. When he wound up a sale, he'd say "So, let's move forward and I know you'll be pleased, Okay?" things would fall apart instead of coming together.

Instead of moving up into a blue sky of hope and optimism, his tone crept down the stairs, into a cellar of darkness.

The end result was that he impeached his own credibility. How can you get someone to feel confident if you're questioning the veracity of the words you're uttering, with a tone that belies them?

Allan, bless his heart, was a genuine misfit, as in misfit for what we were trying to accomplish.

He wasn't cut out to be a lawyer, either, for which he had also studied. Imagine him doing criminal law and he says, "Your Honor, my client, the criminal to my right, is 100% innocent of all charges!"

It's not going to fly!

The point is that our tones and our texts need to be in agreement, they need to reinforce each other. When they conflict, clients and customers are conflicted, and they stall, walk away, or in some cases, they run.

The sage sociologist, Erving Goffman, said there are two kinds of communications, those that are (1) Given and (2) Given-off.

Given ones are intentionally conveyed. We might make ourselves smile as a retail customer walks in the door. But if our mouth is the only thing smiling, and not our eyes, and our crow's feet aren't showing, these expressions given-off convey the impression we are being less than sincere.

We have a default setting for our tones that we use when we repeat certain scripts. Let's take a very common piece of a phone script for reception and customer service work:

"Hello, Goodman Organization, this is Gary, how may I help you?"

Because this is such a commonly used phrase and one that is repeated during the course of a day up to a hundred times, our default setting can be described this way, using my Three T's: Text, Tone & Timing.

We have the Text, written above.

Our Timing is to rush through this line. We say it so quickly that often the words are slurred, forcing people to ask us, "What did you say?"

This wastes time and is frustrating for all of us.

The Tone is especially noteworthy. Just as in my "How do I look?" example, sarcasm, or at least indifference creeps into the conversation.

Most people robotically recite this line, arbitrarily emphasizing the word, "help."

How may I HELP you?

To really sound sincere, they should make themselves emphasize the last word in the phrase, YOU.

How may I help YOU?

(If you're listening to this book, I just demonstrated what I'm talking about. If you're reading it, you'll still get what I'm saying but you should utter these lines the two ways I've suggested, to hear the differences.)

Make the word YOU the highest word in the phrase. It is the top stair in the staircase. Climb up to it, and then utter it as a crescendo.

If it tanks, instead, you're losing a great chance to make a wonderful first impression.

Has anyone ever said to you, "You had me at HELLO?"

This means you made a great impression and people chose to buy at that point. The same applies with the proper intonation of "How may I help YOU?"

I must emphasize the fact that if you go down the stairs instead of up, you'll actually send the opposite of what your words are saying.

Your words are saying I'm ready, willing and able to help, if YOU moves up. If instead your YOU goes down, which it will if you emphasize HELP, then you're signaling:

I know I just said I'm ready, willing, and able to help you, but I lied. I don't want to. My heart isn't in it. Take my tone to be true, not my text.

And just like that, your sales possibilities will vanish in the sarcastic mist.

To underscore this phenomenon, and to add even more practicality to it, let's use tonal analysis to appreciate what happens when we close the deal, Okay?

Let's reach back for that close I used in another example:

So, let's move forward and I know you'll be pleased, OKAY?"

I've capitalized OKAY because this is the word I want to focus on.

Okay is a magical word in selling because if it is uttered just right it will elicit a reflexive Okay from the buyer. We are habituated to answering "Okay? With "Okay."

Okay?

If you're nodding your head, then there you go. It's proof. I do this with seminar audiences all the time and it's funny. We're talking about the power of okay to activate a reflex and most people reflexively respond to okay even though we're analyzing it.

But there's another fun nuance to the word. It is the tone with which you utter it.

You cannot elongate it, as in o-k-a-y. It needs to be said compactly, Ok?

The heavier the deal you're discussing, in terms of money or commitments required from buyers, the lighter your okay sound.

"So, we're only talking two million for the car, OK?"

This needs to sound easy as can be, lighter than air, floating on gossamer wings, bright as a ray of golden sunlight.

The slightest hint of darkness, conveyed by a flat tone or worse, by a descending tone, will abruptly, loudly, and irreversible pop the balloon you've floated, deflating your deal.

At Time-Life, I had a sales rep who was a genius at doing this the right way, and he did it right, deliberately.

What made him especially effective was his earnest and yet measured tone when describing our products. Then he would say, so let's get this book out to you and I know you'll be pleased, OK?"

That OK soared with birds. It was so sweet and optimistic that it made the entire buying proposition seem effortless.

That was the exact meta-message he wanted to convey. There's nothing-to-it-so-let's-do-it.

Had he gone down in tone or if he restrained it on OK in the way he had conveyed the prior text, then he wouldn't have risen to the top ranks of our sellers.

As his tone went up, so did his sales.

It's worth commenting on something else that is a similar phenomenon regarding the correlating between proper tone management and selling.

How loudly should you speak? As your voice grows louder, do you sell more, or do you sell less?

As a communication theorist and as a practical salesperson, I love questions like this! They provide the gist for coming to ever deeper understandings of the connection between subtle message phenomena and our paychecks.

Common sense and our intuition tell us that loud voices are generally offensive while softer tones are more pleasing to the ear, correct?

In a library this is certainly so, and over romantic dinners the same can be said. But when it comes to selling, louder voices generally sell more products and services.

Sales managers know this so well that when they walk into bullpens where stock and commodity traders are plying their wares, if the collective voice level is down so are sales.

Conversely, when voice volume is higher, more sales are made.

This known correlation is listened for and actively managed.

"It sounds like a morgue in here!" or "Who died?" sales executives will bark in their own over-the-top tones.

They may go to say, "Get your voices up!"

You could be thinking that the background noise contaminates other conversations so much that there is a net loss of sales, not a gain.

Noise-canceling headsets, and even conventional handsets minimize background noise, so this really is a non-issue.

Face to face, you don't want to be overwhelming so you might trim back your volume. But you still want to exude confidence in your products, so the principle of having at least a slightly higher volume also pertains to this context, too.

Yet there are exceptions. There should be a certain matching of tones to products as well. Showing your excitement over an exotic sports car with more than 1,000 horsepower is normal.

Gushing over the features of a prepaid burial plan is probably inappropriate.

But remember this distinction. The test of appropriateness is what sells better.

There is a Los Angeles based TV broadcaster who has one of the most unpleasant and raspy voices I've ever heard. I can't bear to listen to him even for the shortest time.

That's me, and obviously this performer pleases his audience, whoever they are. There must be a market for his tones sufficient to support him, his station, and his advertising sponsors.

He's not the only one that doesn't have dulcet tones. There are many more on today's radio stations.

Yet their voices may be EXACTLY right to sell to their audiences. Because they sound so everyday, so common, indeed so rough around the edges, they could be perfect to pitch all kinds of rough and tumble goods and services.

Some make their way into broadcasting sporting events or sports call-in shows.

Above all, what I consider their flaw might be their greatest strength. At least they get people's attention.

The same can be said of effective salespeople. They direct attention to their products in a favorable, or at least we should say, in an appropriate manner.

And once we've listened to them for a while we even get more comfortable with their distinctiveness.

So, be prepared for counterintuitive insights as you assess the meta-messages you're giving-off through tone.

Appreciate the fact that we cannot-not-communicate. Everything we say or don't say will be construed to have a meaning.

And above all, at the meta-level, tones talk!

20

What Is The Best Time To Sell?

Who hasn't heard the expression, "timing is everything?" As with most sweeping statements, this one is flawed, as well. But there is some truth in it when it comes to selling.

We know, for instance, it is potentially problematic to contact people close to the lunch hour. Their stomachs grumbling, or with plans to get some down time in the middle of the day, they may not have any patience for our overtures.

By 4 p.m., especially on a Friday, people are said to depart this terrestrial zone we know, heading off into that gauzy place known as Miller Time.

But in truth, the best time to sell is when you feel like doing it.

My dad was a firm believer in the notion that if you don't feel like selling you won't be any good at it, as long as you foster reluctance. Feel good, and you'll sell well, was his idea.

As I pointed out in my book, *How To Sell Like A Natural Born Salesperson,* dad gave a famous speech at the Wayne Pump Company, where he was their best seller. They asked him to say a few inspiring words that captured his approach.

"Do you see that clock on the wall?" he started. "Forget it! The early bird may get the worm but that's all he gets. Sell when you feel like it, as I do. And if I don't feel like selling, I don't, because I won't."

Quickly this pep talk was moving in a direction his management never anticipated!

"I wake up when I feel like it and have nice, big breakfast maybe at 9:30 or 10. Then I make a call or two, and set up a meeting for that afternoon or the next day. I sell when I feel like it, and that's my secret!"

After being in sales for decades, and having managed and trained thousands of salespeople I can say there's truth in dad's proposition. But of course, if you're a sales manager you'll be inclined to rebut this notion, vigorously.

Instead, you'll push the work ethic to its extreme, saying labor long hours and do all of the extra things your peers won't do, and you'll rise to the top.

Well, heck, talent aside, if Seller A works twice as many hours then he or she probably will out perform Seller B. There are only a few problems with this approach.

For one thing, it isn't sustainable. You'll earn a ton, if the pay plan is decent, rewarding success. But you'll have precious little time to enjoy the fruits of your labor.

Your health may also break down. If that occurs, you'll have to recalculate how productive your mania really was if the price you pay is a lot of downtime because of stress or illness.

Above all, as a seller, you need to know what suits you and what doesn't.

I'm a strong believer in what I call selling styles.

For example, if I'm working a sales campaign and making phone calls, I like to identify a promising suspect and then research them. I'll visit their web sites and Google the names of the key contacts.

Emerging from this endeavor, I'll then ask myself how my services will best meet their specific needs.

Yesterday, I reached out to a solar business. Researching the key contact I discovered he had extensive marketing and PR background with some of the most distinguished global agencies. Also, he had written a recent article on email marketing, which I was covering to a small extent in the class I was contacting him about.

I left him a voice mail acknowledging his extensive background. I said he was perfectly positioned to recommend my program to some key associates, appreciating as he obviously would, the value in its content.

"I know you!" is what I was able to convey, which is a very powerful meta-message. I've invested time to discover as much as I can about you before I called. I did my homework.

Aren't I a clever duck, and don't you want your minions to flock with someone like me?

In other words, my offering deserves your attention in much the same way as I have earned the right to yours.

My selling style is to make fewer but deeper contacts as opposed to many, shallower ones. To me, selling is not an assembly line type of process.

There are few economies of scale we can usher in because one size doesn't fit all. If we're fabricating sales at most it involves what is known as custom manufacturing. The frame of the car may be the same, whether it is a Porsche Cayenne or a VW Touareg.

But after that, the vehicles become distinguishable and distinctive. A Porsche engine is not put into a VW, and vice versa. (Though at one point, the 914 Porsche of the 1970's supposedly ran on a VW power plant.)

In selling, especially today, if we come across as utterly ignorant of the prospect's needs and values, we're quickly jettisoned. I optimize by working in a highly talented and trained manner. It is through using discernment and judgment every step of the way that I make progress in cultivating contacts.

If I want to make a lot of dumb contacts, I should use mailings, press releases, and advertising. Smart approaches operate differently; they're customized.

A few minutes ago I watched a *Wall Street Journal* video about an Italian carmaker who sells possibly a few dozen of his creations each year. They cost over two million dollars, apiece, and they are positioned as 100% hand made works of art.

My ideal selling approach is akin to his method for producing cars. Because I am selling personal consulting, training, and customized seminars, my own, I have only so much "me" I can make available each year.

Operating at peak efficiency I might be able to handle two or three clients each 12 months. So I need to make sure the temperamental fit is right.

If we don't hit it off right away, chances are we never will.

In a very real sense I am choosing my clients as much or more than they are choosing me. Ideally, we'd be able to adjust to everyone and they to us. But that doesn't happen all that often.

An interesting test of this is the T.O. or turnover. Let's say you contact someone and you fail to hit it off. There's a clash right away. You don't like them and they aren't fond of you.

Or they're unduly suspicious. Perhaps we've triggered in each other a memory of someone we really disliked. If you have a T-O capability, which is someone that you've designated to step-in and take over for you, there's a good chance they'll seal the deal where you would have failed.

The simple changing of a voice and the personality that goes along with it can work wonders. I've actually said to partners, "This one needs your gentle touch" before sending a prospect over to a sympathetic ally.

They've said to me, "Here's a guy that is walking all over me," seeking my no-nonsense, tough guy persona.

Just to recap this for a moment, we're speaking about selling styles. Yours may not fit particular prospects, and you should T-O these.

There's another nuance to be taken into account. You may or may not be not be a good mesh with your product. If you're the proverbial 98 pound weakling, good luck selling hard core exercise equipment to serious bodybuilders.

When I was at Time-Life Books, Ben was one of our finest sellers. First of all, he was older and wiser than most, and his voice had a well-traveled authenticity to it. The timber of it said, "I've been there and I know what I'm talking about," but in a friendly, non-superior way.

He also loved books and his other part-time gig was selling them in the building that housed the Beverly Wilshire Hotel. Ben could easily and glowingly talk about books all day and all night. Indeed, that's what he did, and you could tell he was really in his element.

His long-form, or some might say, long-winded style, was a perfect fit with our products, which also went on and on, one book in a library leading to the next.

I was much more to the point. Ben embellished, and his clients loved him for it.

There were really two sales that we were making. The initial order involved getting folks to agree to review on a 10-day trial the lead book in one of our libraries, such as The Cowboys, from Time-Life's Old West Library.

Sellers received a small commission on top of their hourly salary for each lead book sale they made. That was the initial "sale."

But then, the key question, which went straight to the bottom line, was this: Did the people we sent the lead book to actually keep and pay for that first volume?

That was the not quite, but almost all-important second sale. We called it "collecting."

Ben was so-so in the volume of first sales he made. In fact, he may have been slightly below team average in getting trial books out the door.

But his collections were off the charts! All of those extra minutes he consumed waxing rhapsody about the beauty of the binding on the Old West books really paid off for him. And as it turned out, Ben made some of the top money of all sellers because of his collection rate.

Time-Life was smart enough to pay quarters for the first sale, so there was some incentive, but not much. It paid multiple dollars for the collected sale.

So, we're speaking about sales styles, here. Ben's was a great match for Time-Life Books. He knew how to schmooze and create hot anticipation for the first volume, and the same enthusiasm for the second and third volumes that would be sent out, one every other month.

There are some significant meta-considerations implicit in this tale about Ben and Time-Life. One of them is to know thyself, as the portal says at the temple of the Oracle of Delphi.

In this case, I'm saying know thy style. I was and am a hunter. I stalk my sales prey and like to bag them in a swift, clever and bold act. Sure, as I said when it comes to doing my homework, I'll watch their habits, when and which watering holes they frequent. And then I'll pounce.

Ben was more of a farmer. He planted a seed, and watered it by making as many callbacks as it took to fully engage the prospect. And then, the person would ripen into a strong sale in the fullness of time.

Matching these styles to the product is essential. I seriously doubt Ben would have made a good tractor salesman. He would have been wonderful at selling fine art, which also happens to have very nice profit margins.

He sold the Time-Life Library of Art better than anyone else, so I'm not off the mark in postulating this career match for him.

There is a meta-message that a prospect processes when there is a good fit between our selling styles and what we're selling.

At my seminars, when people hear my biography, and then they watch me perform, they comment about how great a fit I am with what I teach. This should be the case with all of us.

Well, with most I would say. If you drive an Uber, very few folks are going to mistake you for being a professional chauffeur. It's a gig! They know it, so they don't expect you to look like a "lifer."

As long as you drive fairly well, they probably don't care what you main squeeze is. How you got to be where you are right now isn't part of what they're buying, unless they are inveterate conversationalists. Then, maybe they expect a little give and take to break the monotony.

21

Small Talk Makes Big Money

There has been an ongoing debate in selling about the desirability of using small talk to break the ice.

"Hello, Daphne? Hi, it's Gary Goodman with Customersatisfaction.com. How are you?"

Some say, it's okay to ask how are you if you know the person. But if you don't know them, it sounds awkward. After all, they're speaking to a stranger and they don't know your motives.

Thus, they don't feel safe in small talking. You're wasting your breath.

Maybe you're better served by getting straight to the point. Which would sound like this:

"Hello, Daphne? Hi, it's Gary Goodman with Customersatisfaction.com. The reason I'm calling is . . ."

But there's still a chill in the air. Plus, you sound like you're on a talk-a-thon, a one way launch with no provision for their input. Blabbing away, without sensing something about their mood, and unconvinced you really have their attention, doesn't sound very promising.

There's no perfect answer, and it's kind of a bind. You won't know how they are until and unless you ask. And if you don't at least try to warm them up, that typically chilly reception may last through the entire encounter.

You could be adding to the frost by not trying to usher in some give and take.

My inclination is to ask, but I alter the wording slightly, because "How are you" can seem too robotic.

"How are things with you, today?" is my offering. It's folksy, which is goes over well in sales, unless you're dealing with a very effete prospect.

The meta part of a warm-up is this: It asks, is this communication channel open?

If people are too busy to talk, they'll interrupt and say so.

But if they're in a decent mood and have a minute they'll respond, "Pretty good, and you?"

"I'm good, thanks."

Then you can carry on, knowing you have earned their attention for another 30-60 seconds.

Asking how things are going enables you to do a little lie detection. Their tones will tell the real story. If they reply, "I'm FINE" sternly, they're saying they're not.

"You sound preoccupied, so maybe I'll reach out another time . . ."

Generally, I don't like feeding objections and excuses to prospects. So, I won't ask at the beginning of a conversation, "Is this a good time to talk?" Or, "do you have a minute?"

But if I have already asked how are you and their voices signal negativity, I may as well toss out:

"You sound preoccupied, so maybe I'll reach out another time . . ."

This inclines them to agree and set me free, or to give me explicit permission to carry on.

"No, I'm just in the middle of something, what's this about?" they may counter.

"I'll make it brief. The reason I'm calling is . . ."

This exchange has enabled me to show sensitivity to their communication needs. This sends a meta-message that says you can trust me to take good care of your business, if you decide to give it to me.

There are lots of folks that would be happy if we could just dispense with small talk, this how are you, back and forth banter. I have to tell them it's not possible, and it's not really desirable.

A little give and take, communicatively, sets a pattern of give and take when it comes to making a deal. Some cultures insist on having extended ice-breaking rituals.

In Hawaii, when I was doing sales seminars through Hawaii Pacific University, I mentioned they could probably speed through the how-are-you-I'm-fine-and-you ritual and get top the meat of the selling proposition.

"Not here," some stopped me. "Here, we Talk Story."

Talking Story is asking how someone is, and after they tell you, you then ask, how are your parents, and Aunt Minnie?

"How are you" is anything but a perfunctory question. It is an invitation to really have a conversation.

In opening up about the activities all of the people in our extended family we send a meta-message of belonging. This will lead to knowing nods and to occasional gales of laughter.

Which puts people into the right mood to buy.

If this sounds quaint and restricted in its effectiveness to remote villages, it isn't. I know a seller in Santa Barbara, a pretty sophisticated community, who grew up there and he lets everyone know this, in detail.

I heard him pitching one fellow he didn't personally know, but knew of by saying, "You may know my uncle, so-and-so. I think he built your garage for you."

He got that sale!

And so it would go, contact after contact. Quickly, he was able to identify with people sending the meta-message that he's a stalwart in the community, a person to be trusted, and supported.

Needless to say, he is a master of small talk.

Not too long ago, I was talking with a prospect in South Haven, Michigan. I recall vividly spending summers at the beach there, with my vacationing family.

Oddly, apart from the lake, what I recall most is the fragrance of the place. It was intoxicating.

I mentioned this to my contact and he said:

"It's the lilacs. We're famous for them. They must have been in bloom near your cottage."

Wow, this secret from Gary's youth was revealed in that quick give and take, that small talk. Through our discourse I revealed myself as a person with a shared history of really having been there.

We become visible and credible as we open up. This is a proven psychological fact. Self-disclosure leads to the formation of trust.

And generally, we need to trust people to buy from them.

What we're doing is creating common ground with people through small talk. It can be about the weather, which used to be an uncontroversial, non-political topic!

I recall speaking to a buyer in Joplin, Missouri, which I traveled through on my way to a teaching assignment in Indiana. The moon was on my left, full and beautiful.

Suddenly, a second moon appeared on my right!

I did some quick double takes while negotiating the pine-ridged highway.

"It's a UFO, I declared to myself, and breathlessly continued on my way.

I told this story to my Joplin prospect and he smiled and said, "Well, we see a lot of strange things up here at night!"

There is a risk in making small talk of this type. You might come across as not fully tethered to this planet! But it's worth the risk because this sort of chat makes you real.

Everyone is a tad goofy. Tap a little here and there, and it will come out and play.

Consider for a moment the opposite of self-disclosure, which is what small talk accomplished. The opposite is concealment.

When we make no effort to open up or we come across as uptight we send a meta-message that we're concealing who we really are and what we're really up to.

This makes people recoil. In fact, they'll mimic our behaviors. If we come across coolly, they'll get chilly, too. This is how defensiveness works.

People are defensive when strangers approach them. It's a self-protective reflex.

Part of that is to imbue the stranger with negative qualities. It isn't our default setting to gleefully think, "Great, I get to speak to a new person today!"

More like, "Do I know you, because if I don't, I don't want to!"

We're familiar with defensive posture, the arms we fold across our chests to protect ourselves. Those arms are armor, and we won't relax their deployment until there are signals that we are not in danger.

Granted, this sounds like an overreaction. If someone has simply dialed our phone number, what do we have to fear?

We can always hang-up. It feels better to fight them in the same way placing a placard at our doorstep that says, "No Solicitors" seems to bestow an additional quantum of solace.

If you're the salesperson, what do you do? You OPEN your arms to wave hello, to signal that you have no concealed clubs to beat them over the head with.

This is what how are you, what small talk, or at least the invitation to make it, sends to the prospect.

If they reject your gesture, well, they're not sellable, at least at that moment. But continuing your talk without checking in with them would have aroused rejection, anyway.

Who knows, your "how are you" might allow them to ask, "What is Customersatisfaction.com?" which is the affiliation you mentioned in your initial greeting.

"Oh, we do this and that, and our clients include many of the Fortune 100. The reason I'm calling is . . ."

In other words, their response could HELP the conversation top proceed, and not hinder it. Appreciate this fact. Sooner or later we're going to need their approval to advance the sale or the relationship.

So, if they're actively participating earlier instead of later, this is okay.

I do have a tonal tip to share with you. When you ask, "How are things with you today: Emphasize the "you."

Punch it out. Give it a little extra emphasis. Doing this, will convey the meta-message you are genuinely interested in hearing their reply.

Plus, it makes you sound authoritative. You may recall this is the way the "enforcers," the boys and girls vice principals would greet us in hallways, at school.

It was friendly, but firm, a way of asserting authority, but being ostensibly friendly.

Remember, there is a BUSINESS reason we're contacting prospects. We're not trying to make new friends, or to develop what I call, phone-pals.

My dad, who was the inspiration behind one of my other books, *How To Sell Like a Natural Born Salesperson*, would emphasize the "how" word in the phrase, "How are you?" From what I could detect, this also works well.

Individuating this phrase or how are things with you, today, is essential to making good small talk, while sending the meta-message that we're safe and desirable to communicate with and to buy from.

22

The Art Of Selling

The Watts Towers are several "backyard" sculptural spires located in the Watts area of Los Angeles. It took Simon Rodia 33 years to construct them.

Using only hand tools, his own cement mix, and cast off rebar and improvised mosaic pieces, mostly broken soda bottles, he personally crafted what have been designated California and United States historic landmarks.

With no formal artistic training and only a day laborer's skills, Rodia did something literally monumental, in keeping with his personal vision of success.

I see salespeople as the Simon Rodias of business. They sculpt communications, persuasive messages that are made from vague outlines, cast off words and other shiny objects that get prospects' attention and move them to buy.

Each presentation is pretty much extemporized, made-up as they go along, including in the process whatever is around in the form of stories, testimonials, facts and figures that seem to be fitting.

Sometimes the result is pure genius. At other times it is good enough, and this approach can also fail miserably.

Rodia's towers have withstood numerous earthquakes and incessant weathering over what in 2021 will mark a century. From a structural engineering perspective, this durability boggles the mind in the same way we can watch sellers in action and wonder how in creation they can succeed.

But it is exactly, in-creation, moment to moment that they do succeed. And many like it this way.

Peter Drucker, who I mention elsewhere in this book, was a management guru and my MBA professor. While waiting for a train from London to Edinburgh I came across his book at a kiosk and bought it.

There is one segment that really caught my eye as a consultant who has spent much of his career teaching salespeople to be better at what they do. It is called the Fallacy of Creativity, and it goes like this:

The Fallacy of Creativity

There is a centuries-old and continually revived slogan of the individual's creativity: 'Free people from restraint and they will come up with far better, far more advanced, far more productive answers than the experts.'

But there is no evidence to support this belief. Everything we know indicates that creativity can become effective only if the basic tools are given.

Everything we also know indicates that the proper structure of work—of any work—is not intuitively obvious.

People have shoveled sand for untold centuries. Most of the time, one can assume, nobody told them how to do it. If making work productive depended upon the creativity of people, they would undoubtedly have found the best way of doing the job before the dawn of history.

Yet when Taylor first looked at the job in 1885, he found everything was wrong.

The amount of sand the shoveler lifted in one operation was the wrong amount, was indeed the amount most calculated to tire him and to do him physical harm. The containers were the wrong shape, the wrong size, and in the wrong position, and so on.

Human intuition and creativity had produced an operation that was both backbreaking and inefficient.

The process was improved by several orders of magnitude by being analyzed and then synthesized again into a single productive operation.

And exactly the same total misdesign of work and process after two thousand years of 'creativity' was found when physicians first systematically analyzed the process of medical diagnosis.

(From Peter F. Drucker, MANAGEMENT, Pan Books)

How does this pertain to selling and to meta-selling?

Sellers love to choose their own tools in much the same way Rodia selected errant pieces of glass and metal to include in his Watts Towers.

But in many cases these tools, like the shovels in Drucker's example, are the wrong shape and size and aren't really optimal.

They aren't optimal in the sense that if you want to shovel the most sand in the least amount of time, while not exhausting or injuring yourself in the process, you're going about it with the wrong tools.

We need to ask ourselves what is the chief aim of sellers? Is it to sell the most we can in the least time while using our energy and attention efficiently?

Yesterday I read an article about a world-class mountain climber who scales office buildings to stave off boredom. The piece mentioned that this climber ascended to the top of some famous mountain peak in a mere three hours.

The first expedition to the top, involving far more gear and personnel, took forty days to accomplish!

On one level, today's rock-star climber is about 320 times more efficient. Wow!

Yet is speed the only thing rock climbers climb rocks for? Is that all there is?

Certainly it isn't, at least for the casual enthusiast.

But we're talking about sellers. Is there such a thing as a casual seller as opposed to a world record breaker?

Let's get back to tools. Much of my work as a consultant has seen me stride into sales units and more or less say:

"Listen-up. You've been using the wrong shovel for way too long. I've designed a better one and I'm going to give every seller here his own, vastly improved copy.

You'll make more money in less time, and that's what it's all about, right?"

What's wrong with this picture?

Lots of things are askew. For one, sellers feel thwarted and inept. They're used to choosing their own tools and heck, what they've used has been good enough.

Moreover, I'm some expert outsider. They don't know me or trust me, or even like me much; certainly they don't like experts and consultants.

And of course they want to sell more, but they also want to figure it out on their own, because that feels better than being told what to do. It makes them feel more grown-up, and smarter if they discover a better way on their own.

With a breakthrough, they get extra credit, and this way, if they accept my shovel it will only make me look good.

On top of this, if they accept outside help this time and it works, I'll be invited back and before you know it, they'll be directed to make more changes, not of their own choosing.

I'll be the sculptor, and not them.

Any monuments that are erected in the form of new sales records and distinctions will have my name on them. Sellers will become anonymous, interchangeable and instantly replaceable parts.

Some of you might be thinking, "This has already happened. I haven't designed my own work. It has already been designed for me."

This is an insight worth discussing.

In many of today's companies sales work is pre-designed. Most jobs I see being advertised are entry-level, meaning the companies doing the hiring are going to pay very little and regiment their people.

Even start-ups without customer bases posture as if they are handing down tried and true processes for making as many sales as possible. Of course, this is a fiction.

They haven't relentlessly scanned the universe for the best sales practices, and they haven't had genuine experts customize programs to their specific goods and services.

They're using an old shovel that is (also) the only shovel they have ever known. It might have been lifted from their last job site, where they sold widgets instead of software or today's leading-edge tech.

But it's new-to-you because you're new to the job and you're going to follow orders. Unless, that is, you're Simon Rodia, and you're going to insist on using your own tools and work at your own pace.

In that case, you'll be a misfit, even if your tools are better.

Here's where I'm going with this.

Ever since Frederick Taylor did his famous time-and-motion studies about the time Rodia started erecting his Watts Towers, so-called "scientific management" has increasingly taken over the workplace. The idea has been to rollout the most efficient ways to scale the bluffs of client resistance, making as many orders as possible.

At least in principle this has been the goal. In reality, selling has been reduced to the industrial revolution goal of "making man work like a machine."

Management has eliminated much of the art from the art of selling.

And how have they done this?

By pretending to know what they're doing and by using dumb scripts instead of smart ones.

We need to have a sidebar conversation about scripting sales calls.

The idea of using a script to sell is the same as choosing the best kind of shovel. A great script can help us to become more efficient, providing it permits flexibility and customization.

The problem is when scripts are used as Lock-Step Monsters, formulas to be used jot for jot, word for word, and tone for tone, without permitting mid-conversation adjustments.

I can hear some of you thinking, "I don't use scripts."

Sorry, you do. We all do. Language itself is a script as is the alphabet. We have a limited number of combinations of letters and sounds we can draw from.

And when we intuit that some choices are working better than others, we repeat them.

These bits and pieces become our Watts Towers of expression.

As long as they withstand the sales elements, customer questions, interruptions, and objections, we not only leave them in place.

We add on to them.

This makes our presentations longer, harder to listen to, and less efficient. But heck, if we're sculptors, what do we care?

This is the crucial fork in the road. We have to make a decision.

Why are we in the selling trade? If it is strictly to earn money, which comes from more sales, then we may not mind working like machines.

Our scripts will tend to be "brief, be brilliant, and be done!" They'll get to the point, and regiment us to march on to the next deal and to the one after that.

But if we're in sales for other reasons, efficiency will be traded-off in some measure to permit other satisfactions to accrue to us.

In another section, I speak of Ben, my best art volume seller at Time-Life Books. He was a talker and he loved to talk about art, museums, anything and everything related and even unrelated to the painters our volumes featured.

Ben was long-winded, and his conversations weren't managed very well for time. At times, I'd stroll past his desk with a knowing smile, and catch his eye with a spiraling finger motion to say, "let's wrap this one up!"

Why was Ben a fixture at Time-Life? What made him catch several buses to reach his place of employment?

Was it the money? In part, yes. We all did pretty well. We were well compensated.

But Ben could have sold anything with his gift of gab. Why did he love his Time-Life customers and why did they love him back?

I mean, it really was a romance that was going on!

Ben's knowledge, aptitudes and abilities, tastes and even idiosyncrasies all came together in making him succeed.

He was the artist and his chats were the canvas, each different, each one a work to be appreciated.

In a word, Ben's humanity came through with every call. Abraham Maslow, an often-quoted psychologist, said we aspire to many things.

We need, at the bottom of the pyramid, food, shelter, and safety.

We also need self-esteem, to feel good about ourselves.

And ultimately, when all of these needs have been met, we strive for what he termed, self-actualization.

This is defined as the motive to reach one's full potential. To some, it is the integration of who we are with what we do.

Rodia was "one-with" his sculpture as he was creating it. In other words, where Rodia's "beingness" stopped and where the towers' started, was not distinguishable at the time of creation.

The self-actualized seller operates in the same mode.

In fact, if you ask salespeople how they feel when they're selling well many will say they're "in the zone" or operating "out of their minds."

The same is said about ballplayers that are feeling so plugged-in that they can do no wrong. Every ball they throw or kick seems to be just right, going where it must go, doing what it must do.

I was selling at Time-Life and at one point in my talk, at a loss for words, I blurted out that describing the book is "like describing a flower with words."

At that moment my improvisation was just what I needed to say, uttered with just the right enthusiasm and sense of discovery that the buyer wanted to experience, as well.'

I made the sale, and the sales room went silent. My manager thought the phrase was terrific, and quite smartly encouraged me to allow more of its ilk to come forth.

Smart scripts allow for these novelties to surprise and delight, and they lead to scripting improvements through innovation.

You should start a meta-dialogue with yourself.

What is my favorite selling style? Is it pre-fabricated or more improvised like the Watts Towers?

Am I willing to trade off more sales for more personal freedom and "artistic" satisfaction?

Do I insist on using my own shovel, or am I open to adopting others if they promise greater efficiencies?

Answer these questions right and you'll not only make a living. You'll make a life.

23

The Power Of Politeness:
Sir, Ma'am, & I'm Sorry

About four in the morning a car ominously sped up behind me on a rural road. I genuinely felt he was going to hit me hard if he kept accelerating. So, I punched the pedal until another lane opened-up.

Suddenly, a light show burst from the roof of his vehicle.

It was a cop! But he wasn't a regular one. This guy was a campus policeman who had nothing better to do than issue tickets on the autobahn that paralleled the university.

Effectively, he entrapped me by speeding up from the rear. Believing he was a nut and I was in danger I accelerated. As it happened, a big rig nearly ran me off the same road several months before, so I was on alert.

"I had you back at the bridge," he said. That bridge was a good mile and a half before he pulled me over. Why did he wait so long? Did he want me to speed up so he could write me up for a bigger infraction?

We went to court about six months later and the judge dismissed the ticket. He also admonished the cop that he was trying to do the Sheriff's job and he would serve everyone better by staying closer to campus.

So, how exactly did I beat this ticket? I beat it not because I'm a lawyer or a silver-tongued devil.

I have a better way of beating traffic tickets.

But first, let me tell you what I do as a matter of course.

I spend a considerable amount of time analyzing the scene. Are speed limits clearly and frequently posted? Without warning, do those limits suddenly downshift from 55 to 25 miles per hour without providing room for folks to gradually slow down?

Was there any exigency that I couldn't help bowing to that prevented me from observing the posted speed limit? Was there any officer misconduct?

Screaming up the rear, unannounced and menacingly definitely qualifies as misconduct, as I see it.

The law may or may not be on my side. The primary reason I beat citations is because I am polite, to a fault. And I keep my mouth shut!

In sales, you've heard about the KISS Method. This stands for Keep It Simple, Stupid! We talk for a living, many of us over-talk, losing deals in the process.

The same applies to beating tickets and staying out of trouble. We should KISS here, as well. But this stands for Keep It Silent, Stupid.

Just last night, I watched a dynamic You Tube presentation titled, "Never Speak To The Police!" This is a lecture that was staged at a Virginia Beach law school featuring a professor and a cop.

Both of them agreed, it NEVER pays off to speak to law enforcement unless you have to. Usually, your Constitutionally guaranteed 5th Amendment right to not incriminate yourself authorizes your silence.

But you waive this right by blabbing. The professor shows how even telling the truth as you see it can get you convicted.

So, I answer very few questions, and I end my replies with sir or ma'am or officer.

"Do you know how fast you were going?" they'll ask you.

If you say "36" or above in a 35 MPH zone, you've confessed to breaking the law.

So, the answer is, "No sir."

That's truthful because your speedometer is not always accurate and who is looking at his dash when she should have eyes peeled on the road?

Officers can easily be twenty years my junior and that script doesn't vary.

I learned this sort of response pattern not in my home as you might have guessed. My parents emphasized showing good manners, but they stopped short of insisting on sirs and ma'ams.

I picked these up in three places: (1) When I did an important U.S. Navy training program; (2) By spending years, on and off in the American South; and (3) In 8 years of formal martial arts training, as a mature adult.

So, I don't argue the law with police at the scene. I don't spill the beans if I have a great defense that will make the ticket go away. I certainly don't "card them" by offering my attorney's identification with my license and registration.

The time to contest the citation is not at the scene. That time will come, after I have rescheduled the court date two or three times, making the officer's memory vague and subject to impeachment.

About two thirds of the time, officers won't even show-up in court. If you're there, you plead not guilty move to dismiss the case.

Without a witness, usually the court complies.

Why don't they show-up? Like most, they take vacations and sick days. You might get lucky with a court date scheduled during their getaway time.

In some cases, I believe they're no-shows because I have been so NICE! In one case, where I was cited for speeding, going 93 in a 65 zone, on my way to Lake Tahoe, the patrolman didn't even turn in the ticket to his administration. Repeatedly, I phoned, and it never showed up in the ticketing system.

When we're polite people will forgive us nearly everything. But when we're rude, they'll forgive nothing.

Building courtesies and pleasantries into selling is ages old. But we forget the power in it.

Again, the culprit is we let success go to our heads. Instead of expressing gratitude through the use of "thank-you," we take on a hard edge of entitlement, jettisoning the common courtesies.

That's a big mistake.

Gratitude and contrition will even revive the dead; dead accounts and prospects, that is.

I was pitching an international fashion-modeling agency a sales training program for its school division. After submitting a proposal, I got no traction whatsoever.

I left message after message, to no avail.

Finally, I composed a letter to the president of the company.

I began with this headline: WHERE DID WE GO WRONG?

I went on to apologize for my sales ineffectiveness.

I said I missed the mark somehow, and considering I teach this stuff I would appreciate their feedback and find it even more valuable than a consulting contract.

Shortly thereafter, the president contacted me and hired me to speak before the entire organization. I must have hit the right note, wouldn't you agree?

I certainly didn't burn that prospect or toss it away. As sellers, a part of the callousness we develop is being able to say, "To heck with that one. Next?"

But some of us don't have an unlimited universe of potential buyers, and we need to exhaust the possibilities before letting them fade away.

Lots of times I have reminded myself to "never cut down a tree in winter." Meaning, the prospect might be dormant, not dead.

Hibernating, so if we let them awaken in the fullness of their cycle, they'll come around.

Politeness pays. People never tire of hearing please and thank-you and when pertinent, those two magical words, I'm sorry.

Even, "I'm sorry I'm such a terrible salesperson" has its place, as we see in this modeling agency example. Though I mention in another section that I like to be dignified instead of seeming pathetic, there is power if you can come across as admittedly, flawed.

Yeah, with all those eager horses under the hood, I let the reins slip and that new Porsche just got away from me. Call me "butterfingers!" I messed-up, I surely did!

If you play this theme correctly, you can win sales through apparent ineptitude. Purposely, you're trying to come across as other than slick.

A famous politician had a reputation for being a little too stuffy. He wasn't simply "one of us," he was better than that. We like leaders that are more politically competent than we are, but in other ways we like them to be the same.

So, at this dinner, he was having a plate of something and then he stood up on his way to the podium. That something he was eating ended up on his shirt and it was bright red.

Smartly, he made a joke about his clumsiness and the crowd loved him for it, instantly warming to him in a way that was new.

This gaffe, this embarrassment and its happy outcome actually have a name in psychology. It is called "The Pratfall Effect," as I mentioned earlier.

Especially if you wear an expert's hat most of the

time, it pays off to show your everyday qualities. This takes the edge off your image and makes it easier to relate to you and to like you.

Add-in politeness and good manners and you're un-beatable.

You can even win after losing, as I did with that agency.

I phoned the auto club the other day to help me to tow my car to the tire store. Early in the conversation, the rep said "I see you've been a member for 8 years. Thank you for that."

I said, "You're welcome. Actually it's longer but I dropped the membership when my insurance included road side assistance."

"A lot of people do that and thank you."

This is a smart script because it injects an opportunity to elicit customer recommitment. I explain in detail how this device works in a groundbreaking book, *Monitoring, Measuring & Managing Customer Service.*

What we're trying to do is to re-sell the client on the wisdom of giving us their business. It may not pay off in a new sale right away, but it anchors clients to us for the long run.

In two months my AAA membership comes up for renewal, so getting me to express pride-in-belonging for the last 8 years almost makes it certain that I'll take it to 9 years, if only to be cognitively consistent.

That customer rep had to pull up my information and verify it anyway. So the added time it took, and cost of our back-and-forth dialogue was nil.

It didn't elongate the conversation. But based on his politeness I did. I offered a joke when he asked if I'd be riding to the tire store with the driver.

"Yeah, I'll be riding up front so please tell him I stick my head out the window and wag my tail, just so he won't be surprised."

He laughed and the call ended very well. They were a little late in showing up, but the pleasantness of their politeness made me cut them some slack.

Being a customer service consultant and a sales consultant, I flashed back to this episode and appreciated the cleverness of the call's construction.

Usually, I place the Recommitment Line at the end and some wise conversational engineer brought it up to the top. Which is to say everything can be improved, even my scripts that have been used more than a billion times.

Figure out how to purposely insert politeness and other pleasantries into all of your sales encounters. Be on your guard about discounting the importance of non-buyers that can still be influencers.

Don't fall into the trap of concluding they don't count if they don't authorize or sign the deals.

Being pleasant to them comes right back to you, lifting your spirits, and your positive attitude will be carried though in your presentations, emails, and voice mails with those that "really count," as well.

24

Doing The Impossible: Selling Without Selling

What if you were trying to sell people and at every juncture they called-out your techniques?

They said, "Congratulations on getting through my administrative assistant and getting me on the line. What did you say to accomplish that? I need to know because we can use that magic, ourselves!"

Somehow, you get past that interruption and they say, "Nice qualifying question! Why waste time if I'm broke or have no authority to buy, right?"

Next, they say, "Good translation of features into benefits!"

"Nice close!" they add. "I love that tie-down: 'So, let's get underway and I know you'll be pleased, Okay?'"

"What a great uplift in your voice, trying to get me to lighten-up and to imitate your optimistic tone! Well done!"

At every juncture they stop you to comment about the techniques you're using.

Isn't this scenario a salesperson's worst nightmare? If every technique is processed as a technique, as a persuasive ploy, every technique will fail.

What would be the only rational response you could make to earn people's business?

It would be the abandonment of all sales techniques. If they're not going to work, if they're doomed from the beginning, what's the good in using them, right?

What would it sound like if you could do this, if you could sell without selling?

In my Introduction to this book I promised to share with you my incredible 20-second sales presentation. I said I would defy you to find the sales techniques in it.

In a minute, I'm going to roll this out.

But let me set this up for you.

A sales technique without announcing itself as a technique is the ultimate meta-selling silver bullet. It is persuasion without persuasion.

Is this possible?

For years, during my early sales career, I thought it was impossible. I mean, if we abandon all techniques, we'll be surrendering our tools. Like a carpenter without hammers and nails and wood, how could we ply our trade?

Flash forward a few years in my development. I've completed three degrees, including a Ph.D. in communication theory. I've taught at the college level for four years while earning those sheepskins, and I need to do something new and more lucrative.

I develop a seminar with the idea of offering it through colleges of continuing education. But to get this going, I have to persuade some of the smartest, stodgiest, and most cynical people in the world, deans and other administrators.

"I can't use the same-old hackneyed sales phrases and techniques with these sophisticates," I recall counseling myself. "If I do, they'll reject me and my courses."

But what would my sales script look like if I stripped it bare of techniques?

Like taking a block of clay and then peeling away most of it until all that's left is spare perfection, I came up with this pitch:

"The reason I'm calling is I've developed a one day program for businesses, the Telephone Effectiveness Workshop, and I was wondering how we might pursue the prospect of offering it at your campus."

Thirty seconds is all it took to utter these words, and they were magical words, indeed. Within 18 months my program was sponsored by 35 universities across the country, many of which would repeat it several times.

I added new courses, and in record time I had developed a durable distribution network for my programs from Hawaii to New York.

All of this emerged from a 30 second non-sales presentation!

I must say, we had somewhat detailed chats after that initial 30 seconds transpired. They'd ask me if I had run it before, what I charged, and if I had promotional materials I could spare.

By the end of that call, we had typically agreed on a target date for presenting the workshop at their venue.

But the sale was actually made without their express approval or conscious realization of it.

The second they started cooperating in describing "how" we would pursue offering the course at their campus, we had already put wind in our sails and were on course for doing it.

The Zen insight I had as I rolled-out this campaign is how we create our own obstacles in selling by insisting on using techniques. Our traditional sales techniques presume that there must be a long exchange of information up front, followed by questions and objections that must be exhausted before we engineer a "yes."

By simply asking for "information" about how we "might" proceed, we turn the conversation over to the other party. And soon enough, predictably and reliably, they sell themselves by answering our non-salesy question.

We bypass entirely "whether" they want to buy in getting them to tell us "how" they buy.

You've heard about these best-selling book titles: *Getting to Yes* and *Getting Past No*, which are part of the negotiation literature. From a Meta Selling perspective, both efforts are wasted.

If we start with yes, if we presume yes, and instead ask how, we are already at our destination.

We don't have to "get" to yes, or "get" past no.

We don't ever ask for permission or set-up failure by presupposing resistance or scripting conversations to overcome it.

If you at all doubt the veracity of what I'm saying, that selling-without-selling is possible, desirable, and incredibly profitable, try it for yourself.

In Florence, I've seen the original statue of *David* by Michelangelo. The sculptor said he "released" *David* from the stone. The figure that has come to delight and amaze millions was already there, trapped inside a prison of block.

If you're doing conventional selling instead of Meta Selling, the goal is the same.

Cut away all of the fluff and verbiage from your sales presentations. Rise above the ordinary. Introduce a higher, better, meta-language into your business encounters.

See what happens.

You'll experience more success than you ever dreamed of.

Afterword

I've really enjoyed sharing this information with you. I hope it will help you to outperform your personal best in selling.

Please let me know how you do!

I can be contacted at the email addresses, and by phone, listed below.

If I can assist you or your company on a consulting basis, present a keynote speech, a customized seminar, or a special training program for you, please let me know.

Best,

Gary

(818) 970-GARY (818) 970-4279
gary@drgarygoodman.com
gary@customersatisfaction.com
drgaryscottgoodman@yahoo.com
gary@negotiationschool.com

Index

A

action language/body language
 defensive, 196–197
 punctuality as, 32–40
Adult-to-Adult communication, 89–90
advertising slogans, 59–65
 book and course titles as, 61, 62–64, 130–131
 of Jerry Della Femina, 59, 61–62
 of General Tires, 60–61
 What we do works!™, 65, 128–133
advertising specialties business selling, 148–149
affirmations, 122, 123–124, 126

Amazon, 152
apologies
 by call screeners, 17
 politeness and, 213, 214
Apple, 113
appropriateness
 in dressing for success, 71–72, 75–76, 78, 81
 of tone in communication, 180–182
arc of sales, 75–78
 motivated sequence of persuasion, 75–76
 sales slump, 77
 success/focus on basics, 76–78
Aristotle, 74
art of selling, 199–208
 elimination of art from, 204–206

art of selling (*cont.*)
   and Fallacy of Creativity
      (Drucker), 200–201
   improvisation and, 207–
      208
   needs and, 207
   outside experts and,
      202–204
   presentations in, 199–200
   scientific management vs.,
      201, 204–205
   tools in, 202–204
ascending tone, 177–179
assurances, 128
authoritative approach,
   15–18, 197
average call length, 100–101
"awfulizing" (Ellis), 123,
   126

B
ballpoint pen selling, 106–
   107, 142–147
Ben (Time-Life Books
   salesperson), 94–95,
   188–190, 206–207
Berra, Yogi, 153
body language. *See* action
   language/body
   language
Boeing, 14, 19
book selling, 51, 66–67, 83,
   94–96, 105–106
business brokerage sales, 165

buying styles
   "No Solicitor" signs and,
      40–41
   "responsible sourcing"
      and, 42–48

C
callbacks, 27–31
   caller I.D. and, 27–28, 50
   "rules" for, 49–50
   "spoof numbers," 28
   voice mail and, 27–31,
      50–51
caller I.D., 27–28, 50
call screening, 13–19
   alternative approach for,
      14–19
   authoritative approach
      with screeners, 15–18
   and Boeing, 14, 19
   classic script of screeners,
      14, 18
   implied privacy and, 17–18
   and mis-shipment pitch,
      144, 145–146
   offering cooperation with
      screeners, 15
   and "smart calls" vs.
      "dumb calls," 166–173,
      205–207
   and Xerox Computer
      Services, 14, 15–19
caps, on commissions,
   104–105

cherry and pit approach,
    88–91
Child-to-Child
    communication, 89
Chouinard, Yvon, 46
client/partner selection,
    82–93
    bad business pushes away
        good business, 86–88
    communication as one-
        way street, 56–57, 87
    80/20 rule in, 83
    ethical issues in, 84–87
    factors in, 82–83
    iceberg theory and, 85–86
    pit polishing approach,
        88–91
    procrastination as signal,
        92–93
    selling style and, 186–187
    Smile Suckers and, 91–93
    Transactional Analysis
        and, 89–90
    tumult as signal in, 91–93
closing
    guarantees and, 65–69
    lead generation separated
        from, 165–172
    power of "Okay" and,
        178–179
    "Sounds good, doesn't
        it?," 64–65
    What we do works!™,
        65, 128–133

cold calls, 54, 136, 146
commissions. *See* sales
    commissions
commitments, meeting,
    32–36
communication. *See also*
    Meta-Communication;
    small talk
    clear and concise, 130–
        131
    "Crystal Clear
        Communication"
        (audio program),
        130–131
    Given vs. Given Off, 176
    language as redundant,
        132–133
    as one-way street, 56–57,
        87
    prompts in, 111–113
    scripts in. *See* scripts
    Three T's (Text, Tone &
        Timing), 109, 176–177
    tone in, 173–182
    Transactional Analysis
        and, 89–90
communicative debt, 17
compensation. *See* sales
    compensation
complaints, customer
    service calls as sales
    opportunities, 108–116
concealment, self-disclosure
    vs., 195–196

conformity
    in dressing for success,
        78–80
    in punctuality, 37–40
consciousness, theory of,
    63–64
consultative selling. *See*
    Level One Selling
contrition, 213
cooperation, with call
    screeners, 15
Cornfield, Bernie, 151, 152
countdown campaigns,
    148–149
courtesy, in responding to
    objections, 136–137
"creative destruction"
    (Schumpeter), 125
Creativity, Fallacy of
    (Drucker), 200–201
"Crystal Clear
    Communication"
    (audio program),
    130–131
customer service operations
    average call length and,
        100–101
    new conversational path,
        129
    as profit center, 108–116
    in retail selling, 162–163
    TEAMeasures™, 129–
        130

D

David (Michelangelo), 221
deadlines, and voice mail
    campaigns, 30
decision-making power, 152,
    160
Deep Work (Newport), 50
defensive body language,
    196–197
Della Femina, Jerry, 59,
    61–62
descending tone, 177–179
dinnertime sales calls, 51
disclosure. *See* self-disclosure
Doors, The, 59–60
Dostoyevsky, Fyodor, 22
*Dr. Gary S. Goodman's 77 Best
    Practices in Negotiation*
    (Goodman), 68
dressing for success, 70–81
    appropriateness in, 71–72,
        75–76, 78, 81
    conformity, 78–80
    "frumpy" approach vs.,
        71–72, 75–76, 81
    "investment dressing" in,
        78–80
    organization and, 34, 79
    in telephone/email sales,
        80
Drucker, Peter, 40, 87, 200–
    201, 202
"dumb calls," 166, 168, 171,
    205–207

E

Ego, 63
80/20 rule, 83
Einstein, Albert, 1
Electrolux, 70–76, 81
elevator speeches, 31
Ellis, Albert, 123, 126
email
    client/partner selection
        and, 91–92
    dressing for success and,
        80
    in following up, 157–158
    "smart calls" and, 171–
        172, 205–207
emotional intelligence, in
    Meta-Selling, 7–8
exercise, as momentum
    changer, 119–122
external urgency, 149–150

F

Facebook, 20
Fallacy of Creativity
    (Drucker), 200–201
feedback
    asking for, 6–7, 8–10,
        20–21, 146–147
    in Meta-Communication
        process, 20–24, 54–57
    from prospects in selling
        process, 54–57
first impressions, 177
following up, 1–2

algorithmic/robotic
    approach to, 152,
    155–156
literature requests and,
    156–157
setting date and time for,
    157, 158
Freud, Sigmund, 63–64
"frumpy" dress, 71–72,
    75–76, 81

G

Gary's Greatest Hits, 14
General Electric, 159
General Tires, 60–61
"ghosting," 1, 156, 158
"Glengarry Glen Ross" (play
    and movie), 164
Goffman, Erving, 176
Google Earth, 5–6
gratitude, 16, 212–213
Great Recession of 2008, 163
group presentations
    and the art of selling,
        199–200
    mind reading in, 25–26
    Telephone Effectiveness
        Workshop (Goodman),
        219–220
    transparency trust in,
        25–26, 139–140
    zone of participation in,
        25–26
Grove, Andy, 130

guarantees, 65–69
  objective, 68–69
  subjective, 68
  "trial" purchases, 66–67,
    98, 99–100, 106,
    188–189

H

Hall, Edward T., 35, 39
Harris, Thomas, 89–90
Hawaii Pacific University,
  193–194
help, asking for, 6–7, 8–10,
  20–21, 146–147
Hobby Lobby, 47
honeycombing process,
  168–171
*How to Sell Like A Natural
  Born Salesperson*
  (Goodman), 184, 198
humor, 140–141, 174–175,
  214, 216

I

IBM, 104–105
iceberg theory, 85–86
Id, 63–64
"If I'm you, here's what I'm
  thinking . . ." gambit,
  21–23
improvisation, 207–208
Intel, 130
intermittent reinforcement
  schedules, 3

internal urgency, 149–150
"It sounds to good to be
  true" gambit, 23–24

J

Jedi Mind Trick, 13
Jobs, Steve, 113
jokes, 140–141, 174–175,
  214, 216

K

"keep-all-over"
  commissions, 106–107
Kesey, Ken, 2
"Kiss Me Kate" (musical), 91
KISS Method, 210–211

L

Land, Edwin, 113–114, 115
leads
  algorithmic/robotic
    approach to, 152, 155–
    156, 166, 171
  distribution of, 164–165
  "dumb calls," 166, 168,
    171, 205–207
  lead generation separated
    from closing, 165–172
  researching, 5–6, 20,
    167–171, 185–186
  "smart calls," 165–172,
    205–207
Let My People Go Surfing
  (Chouinard), 46

Level One Selling
  alternate ways of making contact and, 4–6
  directives in, 3–4
  following up in, 1–2
  Meta-Selling vs. *See* Meta-Selling
  modifications of, 4
  popularity of, 3
  as Smash-Mouth Selling, 4
  as traditional approach, 2
Level Two/Meta-Selling. *See* Meta-Selling
LinkedIn, 20, 168, 169, 171
literature, requests for, 156–157
Lombardi, Vince, 36–37
"Lombardi Time," 36–37
"looky-loos," 154–155
Los Angeles Times
  on identity-theft scams, 154–155
  in "teaser" voice mail campaign, 30
loud voices, 179–180
lunchtime sales calls, 183

M
"Mad Men" (TV series), 59
mail campaigns
  outdated lists in, 170
  save-the-trees pitch in, 170
  "smart calls" with, 169–170, 205–207

Management (Drucker), 200–201
martial arts, 121, 211
Maslow, Abraham, 207
"Meeting Cute," 52–54
Meta-Communication, 7–8. *See also* communication
  about sales resistance, 21–22, 40–41
  in group presentations, 25–26, 139–140
  mind reading in, 20–26
  nature of feedback from, 22–24, 54–57
  with self, 64–65
  What we do works!™, 65, 128–133
Meta-Messages, 7–10
  of advertising slogans, 59–65
  cooperation, 15
  guarantees, 65–69
  meeting commitments, 32–36
  punctuality, 32–40
  "responsibly sourced," 42–48
  self-confidence, 16
  silence as, 55–57
Meta-Persuasion, 7–8
Meta-Sales Voice, 94–96
  and Ben (Time-Life Books salesperson), 94–95, 188–190, 206–207

Meta-Sales Voice (*cont.*)
  "Pratfall Effect" and,
    94–96, 214–215
  "Sales Breath" vs., 135–
    136
  "Silver-Tongued Devils"
    and, 94, 95
Meta-Selling
  alternate ways of making
    contact in, 4–6
  asking for help/feedback
    in, 6–7, 8–10, 20–21,
    146–147
  call screening and,
    13–19
  in changing rules of
    engagement, 10
  Meta-Messages in, 8–10
  nature of, 2
  new technologies-of-talk
    in, 19
  in Polaroid customer
    service/sales campaign,
    108–116
  as "re-animating" selling
    process, 11
  role reversal in, 6–7,
    8–10
  20-second salespitch in,
    11, 218
  voice in. *See* Meta-Sales
    Voice
Michelangelo, 221
Miller Time sales calls, 183

mind reading, 20–26
  in group presentations,
    25–26
  "If I'm you, here's what
    I'm thinking . . ."
    gambit, 21–23
  "It sounds to good to be
    true" gambit, 23–24
  open-ended questions in,
    20–21
  "What are you thinking?"
    gambit, 20–21
mis-shipment pitch, 142–147
  asking for help, 146–147
  call screening and, 144,
    145–146
  names in, 145–147
  self-disclosure in, 144–
    145, 146
  urgency and scarcity in,
    147–149
momentum changers,
    119–122
*Monitoring, Measuring &
    Managing Customer
    Service* (Goodman),
    215–216
Morrison, Jim, 59–60
motivation
  and the arc of sales, 75–76
  needs and art of selling,
    207
  timing of sales and,
    183–184

N

names
  in mis-shipment pitch,
    145–147
  in "smart calls," 168–169
needs, and art of selling, 207
Newman, Paul, 45–46
Newman's Own, 45–47
nonverbal communication.
    See action language/
    body language
Nordstrom, 161
"No Solicitor" signs, 40–41

O

objections, 134–141
  audience anxiety and,
    139–140
  challenges as, 136–137
  courtesy in responding to,
    136–137
  feeding, 192–193
  humor and, 140–141
  mind reading techniques
    for, 20–26
  negative associations and,
    134–135
  and "Obstinate Audience"
    (Schramm), 138–141
  "Sales Breath" and,
    135–136
objective guarantees, 68–69
"Obstinate Audience"
    (Schramm), 138–141

Office Depot, 149
Office Max, 149
"Okay," power of, 178–179
*One Flew Over the Cuckoo's
    Nest* (Kesey), 2
*101 Things Parents
    Should Know Before
    Volunteering to Coach
    Their Kids' Sports Teams*
    (Goodman), 89
Oracle of Delphi, 107, 189
order takers vs. order makers,
    137–138, 161–163

P

Parent-to-Child
    communication, 90
Parent-to-Parent
    communication, 89
Pareto principle, 83
Patagonia, 46, 47
permission selling. *See* Level
    One Selling
Perot, Ross, 104–105
persistence, 9, 41, 57–58
persuasion
  in sales process, 75–76
  and 20-second sales
    presentation, 11, 218
pit polishing approach,
    88–91
"Pleasantville" (movie), 49
"pleaser" voice mail
    campaigns, 30–31

"Poetics, The" (Aristotle), 74
Polaroid, 108–116
    customer service as profit
        center, 108–113, 114–
        115, 116
    history of, 113–114
    tenured employees and,
        113–115, 116
police, and traffic tickets,
    209–212
politeness, 209–216
    apologies, 213, 214
    in asking for feedback,
        6–7, 8–10, 20–21,
        146–147
    in beating traffic tickets,
        209–212
    contrition, 213
    courtesy in responding to
        objections, 136–137
    and customer
        recommitment, 215–
        216
    gratitude, 16, 212–213
    humor and, 214, 216
    influences on, 211
    "Pratfall Effect" and,
        94–96, 214–215
    and re-selling the client,
        215–216
    titles in, 211
"Portlandia" (TV series), 45
"Pratfall Effect," 94–96,
    214–215

presentations. See group
    presentations
price determination, 106–
    107
primacy versus recency, 67
privacy, implied, 17–18
procrastination, 92–93
"Producers, The" (play and
    movie), 75
profit margins, 106–107
prompts, 111–113
prospect(s). See also
    objections
    mind reading with, 20–26
    need for feedback from,
        54–57
    objections of, 134–141
    qualifying. See prospect
        qualifying
    and selling as an
        interruption, 51–54
    signaling of intentions,
        54–58, 153–160
prospect qualifying, 151–160
    algorithmic/robotic
        approach to, 152, 155–
        156, 166, 171
    crystal ball question in,
        154
    decision-making power
        and, 152
    "ghosting" and, 1, 156, 158
    importance of, 151,
        159–160

literature requests and,
156–157
"looky-loos," 154–155
research in, 5–6, 20,
167–171, 185–186
signaling of prospect
intentions, 54–58,
153–160
"tire-kickers," 154–155
punctuality, 32–40
"Lombardi Time," 36–37
professors and, 37
rules of, 37–40
standards for, 39
U.S. Navy and, 38
weather challenges and,
32–36

Q
qualifying. See prospect
qualifying

R
recency vs. primacy, 67
recitation of benefits, in voice
mail campaigns, 31
recommitment, 215–216
referrals, in voice mail
campaigns, 31
resistance. See sales resistance
"responsible sourcing,"
42–48
restaurants, "responsible
sourcing" and, 44–45

retail selling, 161–163
order takers vs. order
makers, 137–138,
161–163
self-checkout terminals
and, 162
trends in, 161–163
Rodia, Simon, 199, 200,
201, 204, 207, 208
role reversal, in Meta-Selling,
6–8, 8–10
rules
for callbacks, 49–50
for punctuality, 37–40

S
Safeway School, 42–44
salaries
base hourly wage with
commission, 98–100,
105–106, 188–190
reasons for, 101–102,
105–106
trends in, 163–164
"Sales Breath," 135–136
sales commissions,
98–107
with base salary, 98–100,
105–106, 188–190
"caps" on, 104–105
independent contractors
and, 103–104
"keep-all-over" variant,
106–107

sales commissions (*cont.*)
    straight-commission
        plans, 98–99, 102–105,
        106–107
    "trailing" variant, 99–100,
        105–106
    trends in, 163–164
sales compensation, 97–107
    commissions in, 98–107,
        163–164, 188–190
    engineering the wrong
        results, 100–101
    salaries in, 98–100,
        101–102, 105–106,
        163–164, 188–190
    "tread lightly" approach
        to, 97
    trends in, 163–166
Salesforce (CRM system), 2
sales resistance
    Meta-Communication
        about, 21–22, 40–41
    and "No Solicitors" signs,
        40–41
sales warm-up, 191–192
sarcasm, 174–177
save-the-trees pitch, 170
scarcity, 147–149
Schramm, Wilbur, 138–141
Schumpeter, Joseph, 125
scientific management, 201,
    204–205
screening calls. *See* call
    screening

scripts
    for call screening, 14, 18
    for customer service
        operations as profit
        center, 108–116
    "dumb" vs. "smart,"
        205–207
    employee refusal to
        follow, 114–116
    as Lock-Step Monsters,
        205–206
    prompts and, 111–113
    Recommitment Line,
        215–216
    and tone in
        communication, 176–
        177
self-actualization, 207
self-awareness
    in Meta-Selling, 7–8
    self-knowledge and, 107,
        189–190, 208
    tone and, 173–174
self-confidence
    with call screeners, 16
    and dressing for success,
        80
self-disclosure
    body language and,
        196–197
    concealment vs., 195–196
    in mis-shipment pitch,
        144–145, 146
    personal background

stories in, 47–48,
    194–195
in small talk, 193–195
transparency trust and,
    15, 25–26, 139–140,
    144–145
self-knowledge, 107, 189–
    190, 208
self-talk, 117–126
affirmations and, 122,
    123–124, 126
awareness of, 119
"awfulizing" (Ellis), 123,
    126
with challenges, 118–123,
    124–126
exercise as momentum
    changer, 119–122
with success, 117–119, 120
thoughts as routines and,
    122–123
Seligman, Martin, 124–125
selling styles, 185–190
cold calls, 54, 136, 146
customization in, 186–
    187, 199, 200, 201,
    204, 207, 208
of lead generators vs.
    closers, 165–172
and "Meeting Cute,"
    52–54
order takers vs. order
    makers, 137–138,
    161–163

and prospect feedback,
    54–57
self-knowledge and, 107,
    189–190, 208
selling as interruption,
    51–54
selling without selling,
    217–221
supply chain
    responsibility, 42–48
T.O. (turnover), 187–188
20-second sales
    presentation, 11, 218
Serling, Rod, 73–74
Shakespeare, William, 91,
    128
show-horse salespeople,
    164–165
signaling, of prospect
    intentions, 54–58,
    153–160
signaling intentions, 54–58,
    153–160
silence
    and lack of feedback from
        prospects, 55–57
    and police interactions,
        210–211
"Silver-Tongued Devils," 94,
    95
Skinner, B. F., 3
small talk, 191–198
    in creating common
        ground, 195

small talk (*cont.*)

"happy talk" in retail sales, 162

in sales warm-up, 191–192

and Talking Story, 193–195

tone in, 192–193

"smart calls," 165–172

email and, 171–172, 205–207

honeycombing process, 168–171

researching prospects, 5–6, 20, 167–171, 185–186

with snail-mail campaigns, 169–170

Smile Suckers, 91–93

"spoof numbers," 28

standards, for punctuality, 39

"Star Wars" (movie), 13

Stiff Them! (Goodman), 62–64

"stinkin' thinkin'" (Ziglar), 124

subjective guarantees, 68

Sumitomo Bank, 103

Superego, 63–64

supply chain responsibility, 42–48

defined, 44

of Hobby Lobby, 47

of Newman's Own, 45–47

of Patagonia, 46, 47

personal background stories in, 47–48, 194–195

of restaurants, 44–45

Safeway and, 42–44

Sutherland, Keifer, 147–148

Sutton, Willie, 51

T

Talking Story, 193–195

"Taming of the Shrew" (Shakespeare), 91

Target, 161

Taylor, Frederick, 201, 204–205

TEAMeasures™, 129–130

"teaser" voice mail campaigns, 29–30

telephone sales

callbacks. *See* callbacks

call screening. *See* call screening

clear and concise communication in, 130–131

client/partner selection and, 91–92

cold calls, 54, 136, 146

dressing for success and, 80

"dumb calls," 166, 168, 171, 205–207

"smart calls," 165–172, 205–207

Telephone Effectiveness
  Workshop, 219–220
*You Can Sell Everything By
  Telephone!* (Goodman),
  61
tenured employees, 113–115,
  116
testimonials, 31, 80, 200
thank you
  with call screeners, 16
  in showing gratitude,
    212–213
Three T's (Text, Tone &
  Timing), 109, 176–177
time-and-motion studies,
  201, 204–205
Time-Life Books, 51, 83,
  94–96, 161, 179
  and Ben, 94–95, 188–190,
    206–207
  and "collecting," 188–190
  improvisation in selling,
    207–208
  sales compensation, 98–
    100, 105–106, 188–190
  10-day trials and, 66–67,
    98, 99–100, 106,
    188–189
time management, voice
  mail in, 27–28, 50–51
timing of sales, 183–190
  dinnertime, 51
  lunchtime, 183
  Miller Time, 183

motivation and, 183–184
selling as interruption,
  51–54
sustainability in, 184–185
in Three T's (Text, Tone &
  Timing), 109, 176–177
urgency and scarcity in,
  147–150
"tire-kickers," 154–155
titles, and politeness, 211
T.O. (turnover), 187–188
tone in communication,
  173–182
  appropriateness of, 180–
    182
  ascending/descending,
    177–179
  emphasizing the "how,"
    198
  emphasizing the "you,"
    176–177, 197
  first impressions and, 177
  humor, 140–141, 174–175,
    214, 216
  managing, 173–174
  matching, 180–182
  power of "Okay," 178–179
  sarcasm, 174–177
  scripts and, 176–177
  small talk and, 192–193
  and Three T's (Text,
    Tone & Timing), 109,
    176–177
  volume and, 179–180

traditional selling. *See* Level One Selling

traffic tickets, 209–212

"trailing" commissions, 99–100, 105–106

Transactional Analysis, 89–90

Transamerica, 86–88

transparency trust, 15, 25–26, 139–140, 144–145

"trial" purchases, 66–67, 98, 99–100, 106, 188–189

trust, 127–133

  assurance as "protesting too much," 128

  showing sensitivity to others, 192–193

  transparency, 15, 25–26, 139–140, 144–145

  and What we do works!™, 65, 128–133

"24" (TV series), 147–148

20-second sales presentation, 11, 218

"Twilight Zone The" (TV series), 73–74

Tylenol, 127

U

U.S. Navy, 38, 211

urgency, 147–150

  countdown campaigns, 148–149

  internal vs. external, 149–150

V

vacuum cleaner selling, 70–76, 81, 159–160

voice, in sales. *See* Meta-Sales Voice

voice mail, 27–31

  callbacks and, 27–31, 50–51

  caller I.D., 27–28, 50

  classic approach to, 29

  "dumb calls" and, 166, 168, 171, 205–207

  "pleaser" campaigns, 30–31

  "smart calls" and, 165–172, 205–207

  "spoof numbers," 28

  "teaser" campaigns, 29–30

  in time management, 27–28, 50–51

volume, of speech, 179–180

W

Wall Street Journal, 186

warm-up, 191–192

Watts Towers (Los Angeles), 199, 200, 201, 204, 207, 208

Wayne Pump Company, 184

weather challenges

  commission sales and, 102

  punctuality and, 32–36

Welch, Jack, 159
"What are you thinking?"
    gambit, 20–21
What we do works!™, 65,
    128–133

X
Xerox Computer Services,
    14, 15–19, 115, 138,
    145

Y
*You Can Sell Everything By
    Telephone!* (Goodman),
    61

Z
Ziglar, Zig, 124
zone of participation, in
    group presentations,
    25–26